Surviving Your Pet's Death

Coping with Your Pain and Helping Your Children

Christine Adamec

The Rainbow Bridge

There is a bridge connecting heaven and earth. It is called the Rainbow Bridge, because of its many colors. Just this side of the Rainbow Bridge, there is a land of meadows, hills and valleys with lush green grass.

When a beloved pet dies, the pet goes to this place. There is always food and water and warm spring weather. The old and frail animals are young again. Those who are maimed are made whole again. They play all day with each other.

There is only one thing missing. They are not with their special person who loved them on Earth. So each day they run and play until the day comes when one suddenly stops playing and looks up! The nose twitches! The ears are up! The eyes are staring! And this one suddenly runs from the group.

You have been seen, and when you and your special friend meet, you take him or her in your arms and embrace. Your face is kissed again and again, and you look once more into the eyes of your trusting pet.

Then you cross the Rainbow Bridge together, never again to be separated.

Author Unknown

Author Disclaimer

This book provides self-help information for readers. It in no way attempts to substitute for or supplant the services of trained animal professionals, such as veterinarians or of mental health professionals, such as psychiatrists, psychologists, social workers and others. In addition, this book provides information on some services or products available to readers, but in no way does the author endorse any products or services that are mentioned. Readers should carefully investigate all providers before choosing to buy their products or engage their services.

Table of Contents

Acknowledgments   ix

Introduction   xi

Chapter 1:   How We Relate to Pets   1

Chapter 2:   People Grieve Differently   11

Chapter 3:   Stages of Grief   15

Chapter 4:   Coping with Your Grief   23

Chapter 5:   When Your Pet Dies Suddenly   37

Chapter 6:   When Your Pet Dies After a Long Illness   43

Chapter 7:   When Euthanasia Is the Choice:
              Dealing with This Pain   47

Chapter 8:   Caring for Your Pet After Death:
              Considering Options   53

Chapter 9:   Helping Children with Their Grief   59

Chapter 10:   People with Special Needs: Disabled
              and Elderly People   71

Chapter 11:   Other Losses: Involuntary Separations
              and Runaways   77

Chapter 12:   When Should You Think About Adopting
              a New Pet?   81

Conclusion   87

About the Author   89

Appendix A: Organizations That May Help   91

Appendix B: Helpful Websites or Bereavement Hotlines   93

Appendix C: Listings of Pet Cemeteries Nationwide   95

Bibliography   107

Acknowledgments

I would like to acknowledge the help of my husband John Adamec, who provided very constructive suggestions. I would also like to thank my sister, Pamela Grahn Sargent, for her helpful comments. In addition, much thanks to my writer friend Dana Cassell for her assistance. Dana is the owner of the Cassell Network of Writers, at http://www.writers-editors.com. I would also like to thank Esther Gwinnell, M.D., a psychiatrist in private practice in Portland Oregon, for her assistance with the book.

Introduction

Maybe you've recently lost your wonderful dog. He always bounded up to greet you when you came home after a long hard day at work, giving you unconditional love and acceptance. He has now died and you miss him terribly. Or perhaps it was your much-cherished cat who died, the beautiful feline whom you and your children chose so carefully together when she was just a tiny kitten at the animal shelter fifteen years ago. She's gone now and you can scarcely believe it.

It could be a dog, cat, rabbit, gerbil, horse, ferret, bird, snake, squirrel or any other type of a wide variety of pets that you have loved and cared for. And now this special animal has died. The common denominator, whatever type of pet you have lost, is the love—and the loss.

You feel so very sad and maybe even devastated. So what do you do? If you're like most people, you shed your tears behind closed doors, in secret, and you don't tell anyone outside your family how you feel. Some people don't even tell their family members about how sad they feel because they think that others may not grieve as intensely (or at all) as they are suffering.

You may not share your feelings because you think that others might regard you as silly or overreacting or even unbalanced, especially if you are sobbing over your loss. But there's another possibility: Other people may have gone through the same inner turmoil when their own pets died, when *they* were afraid to tell anyone about how much it all hurt them.

If you're a man, it might be even harder for you to talk about your grief because real men aren't supposed to become despondent over the loss of a pet, right? No, wrong! But that is the popular perception.

Tim is retired and lives alone after the death of his wife, and he is an avid animal lover. He said he told other men at the fitness center where he works out that he was very upset about the rapidly failing health of Peepers, his pet squirrel. He told them he was distressed about the prospect of having to resort to euthanasia—to putting down poor Peepers. Tom did not meet with positive feedback from the other men at the gym, who either were not interested or who mocked him. These reactions made Tim's emotional pain even worse. He stopped talking about his feelings about Peepers, and he kept them all inside. Nobody wants to be perceived as a wimp or a loser.

This book is for you if you are grieving the loss of your animal companion. This book is to tell you that it is okay, and it is normal to grieve for the loss of a beloved pet. There are tactics and strategies that you can use to cope with your grief and to help your children and others cope too, and they are described in this book. In addition, many anecdotes are offered of the experiences of real people and their feelings about the deaths of their pets. These anecdotes may help you.

Surviving Your Pet's Death is about acknowledging and accepting that it is very sad for many people to lose a much-loved animal companion. The book is also about giving yourself permission to grieve as well as learning to help yourself and others to cope with their grief over losing a wonderful pet.

I have lost beloved dogs, cats and one turtle in my life, and remember them all with fondness tinged with sadness. I hope that this book will help you and your loved ones deal with the death of your pets. I can't take away all your emotional pain, but hope that the suggestions and stories included in these pages may help you.

Christine Adamec

Chapter 1

How We Relate To Pets

Throughout the existence of humans on this planet, animals have been used for hunting, protection, and for companionship. In 1978, a tomb was uncovered in northern Israel that held the remains of a human and a dog who were buried together about twelve thousand years ago. The hand of the deceased person had been placed on the animal's shoulder, clearly indicating the care that someone knew that person had felt for his animal companion during life.

Other experts have made important findings. Archaeologist Stewart Schrever discovered what is considered to be the oldest pet cemetery worldwide located in Green County, Illinois and dating back to 6500 BCE. The oldest continuously operating pet cemetery in the United States is the Hartsdale Pet Cemetery located in Hartsdale New York, and it has been operating since 1896. If you assumed that pet cemeteries were a modern invention, think again.

According to Stephen A. Buckley and his colleagues in their 2004 article for *Nature*, cherished pets were mummified in the reign of King Amenhotep (1400 BCE), including such animals as cats, birds and other pets, and great care was taken with the mummification process of these former animal companions. (Read about a company that performs pet mummification in the United States today in Chapter 8.)

Many types of animals have been in and out of favor through the centuries. For example, cats fell out of favor during the Middle Ages, when people linked them with witches and witchcraft. Too bad! Had there been more cats alive at the time, they might have aborted the scourge of the bubonic plague, which was a disease that was spread by rats. People have long since regained their senses about cats, now popular pets in the United States and other countries.

Perhaps the current era is an especially good time to love a pet. Why? Because many of us are separated geographically from our parents and relatives as well as from the people we grew up with. And it can be a very big cold world out there. Sometimes you can feel like you are just a number. Or maybe you're a lot of numbers. You are your cell phone number, your Social Security number, your ATM number, your credit-card numbers, your patient account number, and undoubtedly many other numbers. You may sometimes feel diminished and unimportant because you are just a number to so many people at so many organizations.

But you're far more than just a number to your pet—this animal sees you as wonderful, great, even godlike! Your pet loves you no matter how much money you make and whether you're on the fast track to success or you're jobless and receiving unemployment compensation. It doesn't matter at all to your pet, the love is there regardless.

To your companion animal, you are the person who feeds and shelters and loves him, and he returns your love back to you, many times over. The most devoted human mother could not continue to offer such unconditional love. In addition, pets don't require a lot of talk (or any talk!) or any explanations about why you did or did not do something. Pets remain at your side, loyally and companionably. They need you. They accept you. They love you.

About 73 million people in the United States were pet owners in 2012, according to the American Pet Products Association. Cats are the most prevalent pets in terms of their sheer numbers (74 million cats), followed by dogs (about 70 million). Dogs are actually present in a greater number of American households than cats because cat lovers often have 2 cats while dog lovers are more likely to have 1 dog. Thus, dogs are present in about 37% of American homes and cats are present in about 30% of homes in the United States, according to the American Veterinary Medical Association.

Grief at the loss of a pet is common, and according to family therapist and retired college professor Froma Walsh in her article for *Family Therapy*, about

85% of people with pets grieve when their pet dies, while more than a third still grieves after six months. Yet this grief does not fit in well with the fast pace of the world today. In our hurry-up world, where we can bank and eat on the run using drive-through windows, while we intermittently text others on our cell phones, it's easy to assume that most problems should be resolved quickly and efficiently. After all, if I can email people in other countries and send and receive faxes to them on the same day, then why couldn't I—or you—deal quickly with most other problems?

Here's the thing. When you form a deep attachment to an animal or to a person, it's not readily given up. There's no easy reset or delete button for you to push to rid yourself of those messy unpleasant emotions. Nor can you realistically limit your grieving to an hour or a day—your emotions can't be so readily programmed or unprogrammed. But there are ways to help you with the grieving process, and this book offers suggestions and strategies.

People And Their Animal Companions

Why do people care for and love pets? One obvious motivation is that they love animals. In addition, if they have children, they may want to teach their children to care for and love animals too—as their parents also taught them when they were children. Studies have shown that mothers who had pets during their own childhood are more likely to also have pets in their adulthood–when compared with mothers who did *not* have pets during their childhood. Caring for an animal can give a child a feeling of competency and responsibility. Children also really enjoy the unconditional love and acceptance that they receive from their pets.

Pets also enjoy human companionship. My cat looks forward every day to when my grandson Tyler arrives home from school, and as soon as she hears him shout "Fluffy!" she bolts for the front door. She also frequently watches him in the window as he leaves for school in the morning. In addition, when I say to Fluffy, "Go find Tyler," she races off to search for him. They have their own unique human-animal bond.

In most cases, pets are very special to their human companions. As a result, when a much-loved animal with these prized qualities dies, it is also the loss of their unique traits that causes the human companion to feel emotional pain.

The Role of Pets In The Family

People interact with and relate to their companion animals in very different ways. Some people treat their pets as family members. The pet sleeps with them, goes on trips with them, and generally shares their lives. For others, the pet is more like a friend or even a sibling. In this section, I cover some of the roles that pets may fulfill in the lives of their human companions. Your pet may have fit one or several of these roles in your life or in the lives of your other family members. You may also be able to think of other roles that your pet fulfilled for you and your family members.

Role: A Friend

Your animal companion may serve as a friend who provides love and comfort. Some of Doctor Smith's patients are occasionally startled to notice a black Labrador retriever dozing on a rug in the doctor's back office. The doctor rushes around from room to room seeing many patients all day long and periodically darting over to the hospital for an emergency or to perform surgery. But he always takes a little time to talk to his dog and check on whether she needs anything. On a tough day at the office, he says it's a relief to see that she's still there and still waiting for him. Human friends may move away, get angry with you and break off their friendships or take any number of actions that distress you. But your animal companion is a faithful friend for life.

Role: A Family Member

Some people consider their animal companions to be active members of the family. They talk to them frequently and the animal is often at their side, sometimes so close that they seem like an extra appendage. If they go on a trip, the animal comes too. Tom considers his dogs as part of his family and says, "Dogs repay our care of them with total devotion. I don't really care where they are on the evolutionary chain."

In *Pet Loss and Human Bereavement*, author James M. Harris describes a woman who arrived for a scheduled therapy session sobbing. The therapist asked her what was wrong and she said that her cat had just died. The therapist said she was sorry and the patient replied that the therapist didn't really understand. "She was just like my own fur and bones," said the grieving patient.

Role: A Child

Some pet caretakers treat their pets like their children, and they enjoy caring for them and even babying them. They may buy or make special gifts for their pet or clothes, such as sweaters or hats. In fact, some pet owners have reported on a new love interest of theirs who did not like the pet at all. When the other person said to the pet lover, "That pet has got to go. It's him or me," it was the pet that stayed.

Role: Pets as Siblings

Sometimes animals are seen as a sort of sibling to a human child, if the primary caretaker is a parent. In fact, there can be some "sibling rivalry" if the parents seem to pay too much attention to the pet and not enough to the child. One college student complained that when he came home from school on breaks, the dog still received all the best leftover foods, not the young man. He was mildly aggrieved, but he also laughed about it, taking it in stride. Because he loved the dog too.

Role: Pets as Recreational Companions

Sometimes an animal companion is important to you because he engages in physical activities with you—playing ball or running about, and he may even drag you out of your old easy chair when it's time for a walk, thus giving you the side benefit of some much-needed exercise. (Read more about the health benefits of animal companions later in this chapter.)

Pets can be extremely important to children, and many children enjoy the companionship and playfulness of their pets. Playing with the pet allows the child to get rid of any excess energy and stress left over at the end of the school day. It also enables the child to think about the needs of someone else.

Often when a pet dies, and for some time afterward, pet caretakers report that they automatically reach for the pet's leash at the regular walk time or they unthinkingly listen for the animal's familiar noises. Then they remember that their animal companion died, and feel sad and possibly even a little silly. Yet these are normal reactions of grieving pet owners.

Role: Pets as Projections Of Yourself

In some cases, the pet owner strongly identifies with the features and personality of an animal companion, either as the owner perceives him or herself to be or wants to be. For this reason, a young man who chooses a virile and healthy male dog may be loath to have the animal neutered, just as he himself would not want his sexual desire and fertility shut off.

If you perceive your pet as an extension of yourself, then the pet's death can be very traumatic, and you may feel like a part of yourself has died too.

Role: Pets as Transitional Objects

Some experts have suggested that a pet serves for children as a sort of "transitional object" to adulthood, somewhat similar to the teddy bear or blanket that is so important to the preschooler. In this respect, the pet may also be very helpful to adolescents. No self-respecting teenager can get away with carrying around a beat-up old teddy bear or a torn blanket that was loved since infancy—but they can hug and pay plenty of attention to their companion animal.

Role: Pets as Stress Buffers

The mere presence of a pet can help people "get through" the very difficult times that can occur in life, such as a job loss, a move to another city, a divorce, a serious illness, a child going away to college for the first time and so forth. In addition, even in the good times, receiving love from your companion animal as well as giving love to your pet can be emotionally calming and rewarding. As a result, when the pet who eased your stress levels dies, you may feel at a loss, knowing that your pet will no longer be able to provide you with that loving support. Your stress buffer is now gone.

People in the Same Family Have Different Relationships With Pets

If you have more than one person in your household, then there is probably more than one human-animal relationship going on. One person may baby the companion animal while another may take the pet for runs and exercise. A third person may ignore the animal altogether. In turn, the pet will relate to these humans in different ways, attracted more to some than to others.

As a result, when a pet dies, the intensity of grief and the way the grief is shown, varies among family members. Some will openly grieve. Others will care deeply, but will try to hide or repress their feelings. And others will be sad but will not actively grieve. Even family members who didn't like the pet that much will be at least somewhat affected.

Being aware of these various roles can help us understand why pets are so important to us in life and why we are so saddened by their deaths.

Health Benefits To Pet Ownership

It has been proven in many studies that having a pet can improve your health and decrease your risks for some chronic serious diseases. In an analysis of numerous studies on the health benefits of the human-animal bond, the researchers Erika Friedmann and Son Heesok cited research in which the mental and physical status of people who adopted a pet from an animal shelter were compared to the mental and physical status of non-pet adopters over six months.

The researchers found that the pet adopters had significantly fewer health problems than the non-adopters, such as fewer painful joints, fewer headaches and less cases of hay fever. The pet adopters also experienced a significant decrease in pre-existing mental health problems after adopting their pet. Other studies have found that pet ownership significantly decreases an individual's stress rates.

The list below cites a few health advantages of having a pet in your life:

- Lower blood pressure
- Lower cholesterol rate
- Lower triglyceride rate
- Faster recovery from hospitalization
- Improved concentration
- Weight loss
- Decreased levels of depression

Studies on Human Health And Pets

One study looked at the health of cat owners only, and the researchers found that the risk of fatal cardiovascular events, such as a heart attack or a stroke that led to death, was significantly lower among cat owners when compared to those who didn't own a cat. The researchers compared 2,435 cat owners to 2,000 people who had never owned any cats. The findings were published by Adnan Qureshi, M.D. and colleagues of the University of Minnesota in Minneapolis, Minnesota in a 2009 issue of the *Journal of Vascular and Interventional Neurology.*

The researchers stated that having a cat as a pet could be a novel strategy for preventing cardiovascular disease among those individuals who were at high risk for this type of disease.

Pet Grief is Hard For Some People To Understand

With all the many reasons for becoming attached to your companion animals, why is it that so many people just don't understand why a person would mourn a pet that has died? I think that this lack of compassion could be missing at least in part because the baffled person has never had a pet or if they did have a pet in the past, he or she did not feel deeply about the animal. It's not necessarily that they are uncaring or mean people. They truly just don't "get it." No matter how hard you try to explain how you feel to them, you probably will be unsuccessful.

Table 1.1 offers some statements that are sometimes made to individuals who are grieving for their animal companion and includes some possible responses for you to consider in response. Also included are responses that you might think to yourself, but you should generally *not* use. (They are offered because they may be the first thing some people might think in their minds, but hopefully not say.) Use the chart as a guide and tailor it to your own needs.

Table 1.1: Comments People Make in Response to Your Bereavement Over Your Pet's Death and Your Possible Responses—and What You Should NOT Say

Comments People Make	Your Possible Responses	Responses You Might Wish to Say—But Don't Say Them!
Why don't you go on a vacation and get your mind off things?	Being at home is comforting.	Did you go on a vacation right after your wife died?
You should get another (dog, cat, etc.) right away.	I loved my pet and no one could ever replace him. Maybe I'll get another pet someday, but I'm not ready now.	Maybe you should mind your own business.
Why don't you take on some new projects and keep yourself busy so you don't have time to think about this?	I'm grieving and can't handle new projects right now.	What did you have in mind? (And then find fault with each suggestion.)
You need to just snap right out of this. You have to stop dwelling on the past.	Grieving takes time.	I'm not a robot, I'm a person.
My grandmother lost her dog so I know exactly how you feel.	Grieving is different for everyone.	So you could read your grandmother's mind to know exactly how she felt? Can you read my mind too?
You should be fine in a couple of weeks.	It'll take as long as it takes. There's no schedule for grieving.	Sure. My pet was only my best friend for the past ten years.
You're really freaked out about this. Can't you take a pill for that?	I guess it's hard for you to understand.	Is there a pill for curing a cold heart? If there is, *you* should take it.
Let me know if there's anything I can do to help.	Thank you.	Leaving me alone would work.

Don't waste your time trying to convey your feelings to people who are clearly baffled by them. Instead, talk to other animal lovers, who can give you the empathy and support you need. Try not to take offense with those who don't understand how you feel, and realize that in many cases, people thoughtlessly toss off comments, not trying to send a verbal arrow through your heart.

People grieve differently, with some experiencing the loss of a pet far more intensely than others, and the next chapter discusses this issue.

Chapter 2

People Grieve Differently

Because of the many different personalities, ages, and outlooks of pet lovers, when a companion animal dies, their human methods of grieving and the intensity of that grief may vary considerably. Children may also grieve very differently from adults.

I remember when I was about 10 years old, my pet turtle Greenie died and I was very sad. I suspect that my father may not have been too broken up by the death, but to his credit, he was very sensitive to my feelings. He found a little box for my turtle and told me that we would have a burial ceremony in the backyard. He dug a hole and gently placed the box in the ground, covering up the box holding my little green turtle with the dirt. My sister, father and mother came to watch, and my sister and I cried. But it felt right to honor Greenie. Afterwards we talked about the time when Greenie escaped, and we all frantically searched for him, finally finding him hiding in the bathtub.

There is no one "right" way of grieving over the loss of your pet, and it's important for family members and friends to understand that. The person who suffers in silence may resent the person who cries publicly, seeing him or her as hysterical, while the person who is openly upset may see the quietly grieving person as someone who is an unloving and uncaring person. Yet some people are very adept at hiding their emotions.

Acceptance of your own feelings, whatever they are, and acceptance of the feelings of others when they lose their pets, will help you and the entire family unit. It is very unreasonable and unrealistic to expect everyone in your family to feel just as you feel. They can't.

Factors Affecting Intensity Of Pet Grief

Research has demonstrated that some factors increase the intensity of a person's grief when a pet dies. The more attached that a person was to a companion animal, then the more grief he or she will feel when the pet dies. There are also other factors that can exacerbate the grief levels, based on research studies. For example, individuals who live alone or with one other adult are more likely to grieve more intensely when their pets die than families who have three or more members living together. People who are socially isolated or who are under severe stress are also more likely to suffer serious grief when their pet dies than others.

Help From The Vet

In the results from a study published in the *Journal of the American Veterinary Medical Association* in 2000 of 177 clients from 14 veterinary practices in Ontario, Canada, all the clients had experienced the recent death of a cat or dog. The researchers Cindy L. Adams and her colleagues found that about 30% of the clients suffered from severe grief.

They also found that the greater the level of attachment to the pet had been, then the more intense the grief that was suffered upon the animal's death. In addition, the study revealed that professional support received from the veterinarian's office was another factor in the intensity of grief: Support from the veterinarian and staff helped to decrease the person's intensity of grief. In a finding that is not surprising, people who said that they felt like murderers for having their pet euthanized subsequently suffered from more intense levels of grief than others who did not have this belief.

In a small study of 18 recently bereaved pet owners in Japan, published in 2011 in the *Journal of Veterinary Medical Science*, the researchers Yuya Kimura and colleagues reported that the following factors increased the risk for depression or neurosis after a pet's death:

- The age of the deceased pet (younger pets who died increased the person's risk)
- The age of the human companion (those younger than age 35 were at greater risk, possibly because older people are more likely to have previously experienced deaths of pets and humans)
- Family size (the fewer the family members, then the greater the risk for a problem)
- Families whose pets primarily lived *inside* the home had a greater risk

This does not mean that if your pet was elderly or you are an older person or a member of a large family or if your pet lived mostly outside that you can't be upset when your animal companion dies. Of course you can be. It simply means that the study indicated that the risk was exacerbated among members of other groups.

Support And Understanding From Family And Friends

Other studies have found that support from your family and friends decreases the risk for anxiety and depression among bereaved human companions. It is not that others somehow take all the grief away, but rather that their understanding of the loss makes it more tolerable. However, sometimes support is *not* present because family and friends may not understand the deep sadness many people feel with the loss of their pet.

Your Past Life Experiences

Past life circumstances may also affect the person's ability to deal with a pet's death. For example, if other family members such as a parent or a sibling have recently died and then the pet dies too, this can feel like a "piling on" effect of negative experiences to the individual. In contrast, if the person has never experienced the death of anyone before, as in the case of most children, the death of a pet can come as a major shock. Parents need to acknowledge and accept that their child is very sad. (Read suggestions about helping grieving children in Chapter 9.)

Your Past Experiences With Your Pet

Sometimes it's the experiences that you have undergone together with your pet that can cause a strong bonding and thus intensify the grief when the animal companion dies. Frank, a physician and a pet lover, was on a camping trip when it became extremely cold and he could see that his beagle Charger was in danger of dying. He took the dog into his sleeping bag with him all night and his body warmth enabled Charger to survive. This experience bonded the man and dog together, and they were thereafter inseparable. Several years later, when Charger died, Frank was devastated.

When my beautiful black Labrador retriever Missy died several years ago, I thought I could handle it because I was tough. But when I started thinking about Missy and the past we shared, I began sobbing. I remembered what a good dog she was, always leaping up and warning us loudly when someone was at the front door and before the person even had time to ring the doorbell. I remembered her romping with my younger son in the backyard and also remember when he was a small child and held the dog on a long leash as he roller-skated up and down our street with me watching. So many memories! Thank you, Missy.

Some people say that they were drawn to their pets because these pets hated everyone else but them, thus singling out the pet owner as a special person who was worthy of affection. It is hard to deal with the death in that case because that special bond has been destroyed. In other cases, the animal itself was perceived by others as very unattractive and rather ill-tempered, and their human companions said that no one else would ever have loved this animal but them.

Grief may be manifested in many different ways, and many grieving individuals pass through specific stages of grief. This is the subject of the next chapter.

Chapter 3

Stages Of Grief

*J*ust as you suffer from the death of a beloved person, you may also experience different stages of grief when your companion animal dies. You may experience some or all of these stages and they may or may not occur in the order that is described here. However, knowing about the common grief stages may help you with your grieving. This chapter also covers the physical and emotional symptoms that can accompany grieving your loss, and talks about people who seem to be "stuck" in their grief.

The Five Stages Of Grieving

Elisabeth Kübler-Ross long ago attempted to explain key grieving stages that people often experience with major losses, and others have expanded or redefined her explanations. I'll discuss here the five key stages that humans may go through when a pet dies. These five grieving stages include denial, anger, bargaining, depression and acceptance.

Denial Of The Problem

Denial is a very common stage of grief. You feel like this awful thing could not have happened—it's so terrible that it can't be real. There may be a feeling of shock and numbness. Dr. Jones, a veterinarian, reported that after telling a woman that her animal was terminally ill and would die soon, the pet owner kept insisting to the baffled vet that he must trim the dying cat's claws. The woman was not ready to deal with the imminent death of her pet, and she was revealing her denial of the problem very clearly to the vet.

Denial isn't necessarily a bad thing—it's one way that we humans have of initially coping with severe problems until we have a chance to prepare ourselves emotionally and intellectually. It's when we never—or for a very prolonged period—accept the reality of a situation that denial becomes problematic.

A complicating factor can be that the human companion to the animal just never really thought about the death of a pet, and seemed to think that the pet would live forever. When the animal does die, this loss comes as a severe shock. It wasn't really that the person thought the pet was immortal. It just was presumed that the pet would always be there, as a sort of "given."

Anger

Anger is another grieving stage that many bereaved people may pass through. You may become unreasonably angry at another family member or wish to blame someone else for your pet's death. Some people blame the veterinarian, often unfairly. You may think that the vet should be able to heal your animal. Try to keep in mind that veterinarians are animal lovers who usually try to perform their best. But they cannot always succeed in healing the animal, nor do they have power over life and death when an animal is very sick.

Janine said that after the loss of their ferret Frankie, whom she and her husband both adored, her husband Jim went a little crazy. "Jim was violently angry. He pounded the side of our van with fists after we lost Frankie, and he cried his heart out. He also made idle threats against the vet, was unspeakably moody with me for days, and was sulky at work."

Sometimes people get angry with God for taking the pet from them. Or their anger is turned inward and transformed into guilt, as they think of the multitudes of things that they either "should" or "should not" have done. Often there was no way that you could have prevented your pet's illness and/or death.

In some cases, you may even be angry at the pet itself. For example, maybe he ran into the street and in front of a car and was hit and killed, although you had previously yelled at him about a hundred times before to not do that. You are also angry at the pet for leaving you. These feelings are irrational. But they are also very common.

Bargaining With Yourself Or Others

Another grieving stage which may occur to someone who has lost an animal companion is the "bargaining" stage. This stage usually occurs if the animal is seriously ill but hasn't yet died. The caretaker may try to bargain with God or may promise herself that she will always and forever be good if only somehow the pet will continue to live. She will buy only the best pet food. She will pay lots more attention to the animal. She will be the best caregiver that is possible. The problem is that death comes to all animals (and people), no matter how wonderful their human companions are or how attentive and loving they are.

Depression

The sadness and "down" depressive feelings that often occur when your animal companion dies are common emotions. Cathy described her past relationship with her cat Spot, and the grief that she felt at his death. "I have to say that this was the most important loss in my life. His death saddened me more than even my parents' deaths. This cat brought me back from a very hard time in my life and he gave me reason to live at one point. His suddenly being gone just seemed unbelievable and insurmountable."

She did, however, get beyond this pain eventually, and Cathy wants others to know that it does get easier to bear over time. "There are moments when you think you'll never be normal again, but time corrects that eventually. There will be a time when the sad memories are replaced by the ones that make you smile and that brighten your day," she says.

The depressive stage of grief is not the same as a clinical depression; however, some people do become clinically depressed from grief when their pet dies, and if symptoms persist, they should be treated. According to the National Institute of Mental Health (NIMH), a clinical depression may be characterized by the following signs and symptoms:

- Persistent anxious, sad or empty feelings
- Feelings of hopelessness

- A lack of interest in past activities that were pleasurable
- Sleeping too much or not enough
- Eating too much or not enough
- Thoughts of suicide or attempted suicide
- Headaches, cramps or digestive problems that are not relieved by treatment
- Decreased energy and fatigue

Note: Anyone who has thoughts of suicide, a plan for suicide or who has attempted suicide urgently needs to see a mental health professional. Depression is very common and very treatable. Depression is treated by therapy and may also be treated with antidepressant medication.

Acceptance

When acceptance of what has happened occurs, as in the fifth stage of grieving, the person may still feel distressed—"acceptance" doesn't necessarily mean that you're totally okay with this loss. Instead, you may still be sad about it. Talking to sympathetic others can help.

With acceptance, you can focus more on the good times that you and your pet shared together. Said one bereaved human companion, "I'm starting to get to the point where I can laugh about all the funny things she once did—and there were so many of them!"

Symptoms And Expressions Of Grief

What really surprises and sometimes distresses or baffles numerous people is that many of the same emotions that they feel when a valued person dies are also experienced when a beloved companion animal dies, such as severe grief and even depression.

Note that it is important to differentiate grief from depression. These emotions may feel like they are very much alike—but they're different. With depression, you feel the world outside is okay but there's something wrong or sick or bad inside you. You may even feel like the world might be better off without you. Conversely, grief is a deep sadness that has to do with a loss that occurs from the outside. You feel very bad but you may or may not also be depressed.

Many people cry over the loss of their pets, and veterinarians say that grown men may cry like babies when their beloved dog, cat or other pet dies. You may find yourself feeling preoccupied with thoughts of the pet and drawn to objects and toys that were familiar to the animal, such as your dog's leash or your bird's favorite toy. Some sounds may remind you of the pet, such as the meowing of a cat outside. Some smells may remind you of your pet too—the smell of the pet may still be on a favorite blanket or object. (And you should be careful about immediately throwing out every item associated with or used by the pet—keeping a few items for a while can help ease your emotional pain.)

Emotional Symptoms

Your emotional health may be greatly affected by the death of your companion animal. You may feel extremely lonely. You may feel restless and unable to sit still, but you don't really know what to do. You may also feel disorganized and confused; for example, you may find it impossible to finish a task before your mind wanders off.

Some bereaved pet owners worry that they are actually losing their sanity, particularly if they have never faced a major loss or grieving situation in the past. Yet only rarely are these fears justified. In general, we don't talk about pet grief much in our society, and as a result, many people have no emotional yardstick with which to evaluate their emotions when a pet dies.

You may catch yourself searching for the animal in its usual past places. "I still keep looking for Merlin," said Tina of her boxer. "He was always my dog, always just about attached to my side. I miss tripping over Merlin because he had to be as close to me as possible in whatever room I was in." Some owners have stated that they even unconsciously try to avoid stepping on the absent pet. You may also imagine that you see or hear your animal—you have not lost your mind if this happens a few times. It's a common grief reaction.

Other psychological reactions may include those listed below.

- Confusion
- Helplessness
- Anxiety
- Panic
- Fear

- Shock
- Sadness
- Drop in self-esteem
- Guilt and self-blame
- Numbness

You may experience some, all, or none of these feelings. The death of a favorite pet can also bring back memories of your other pets that were loved and lost in the past, and may also bring back memories of deceased people who were very dear to you, such as your parents, grandparents, other relatives and friends who have passed on. If your pet died of cancer, it may bring to mind family members who have also died of cancer.

Let's explore just a few of these symptoms, including panic, a drop in self-esteem and guilt and self-blame.

Panic

When you realize suddenly that your animal companion is very ill or even dying, you may feel panicked. Help! What do I do now? You may freeze up and be unable to take any action until the panic subsides sufficiently. Or you may rush around the house, still not doing anything except moving because you don't know what to do. This level of panic is understandable and it's normal. Don't beat yourself up about it if it happens to you.

A Drop On Self-Esteem

After the death of your animal companion, you may find that your self-esteem has plummeted. You may think that someone else would have done things differently and better than you, thus resulting in your pet's still being alive today. You may even think that you are a bad person because of something that you did or didn't do regarding your pet.

Yet no one who loves animals would willingly harm them. Even if you indirectly or directly somehow caused your pet's death, it was never your intention to hurt your animal companion. If it helps, tell your pet that you're sorry. Some people say that it helps to say the animal's name aloud several times.

Guilt And Self-Blame

You may also be guilt-ridden with the "what-ifs" or the "if onlys." If only you had locked the cat out of the porch, where she never went anyway, then in that split second when you turned your back, your cat wouldn't have been able to kill your pet lizard while it was sunning itself. Or if *only* you had remembered to give your pet that pill three weeks before she died, maybe she wouldn't have become sick and died.

If the animal dies at home, the owner may think that he or she should have brought the pet to the animal hospital. Conversely, if the animal dies in the animal hospital, the person may think that the pet should have died at home where he was happy. It's a lose-lose type of thinking, but it's also very common.

Hopefully, your veterinarian, family, friends, and others will remind you of all the loving care that you have provided for your animal, maybe for many years. Listen to them! And try to forgive yourself for any errors that you may have made. Don't search for reasons to blame yourself, and don't listen to others who may want to assign blame to you.

Physical Symptoms Of Grief

Along with your emotional responses to the loss of your pet, you may experience physical symptoms as well. You may have respiratory complaints, such as short-ness of breath or hyperventilation (rapid breathing). Barry told me that within hours after his dog Blue's death, he arrived home from the veterinarian's office and started hyperventilating. He was afraid that he would fall down, so he lay down on the kitchen floor until the feeling had passed, and he felt like he could again stand without risking falling or fainting.

Some people who lose their pets have gastrointestinal difficulties and develop stomachaches or diarrhea. If these symptoms persist, see your doctor.

Examples of some physical symptoms that may accompany your bereavement at the loss of a pet may include:

- Diarrhea or constipation
- Light-headedness
- Shortness of breath
- Extreme tiredness
- Stomach pains

Sometimes the symptoms that you experience as a result of your bereavement can lead to other health problems. For example, the diabetic who is not sleeping enough and who is eating irregularly (or not at all) because of grief runs the risk of developing low blood sugar, also known as hypoglycemia. This is a potentially dangerous situation. It is still important to take your regular medications and, if you are a diabetic, to test your blood so that you can react to the findings of low or high blood sugar.

If you have hypertension, don't stop taking your medications, because you could become very ill. Continue treating any other chronic or acute health problems that you have been diagnosed with and taking your regular medications unless your doctor advises otherwise.

It may not seem like it's important to do so when you are grieving, but it *is*. Certainly your pet would not have wanted you to make yourself sick with grief.

If You Become Stuck In Grief

In some cases, people become terribly distraught and they cannot seem to overcome their grief. Sometimes the grief may be tied in with other losses from which they have suffered. For example, one woman who was completely bereft about the loss of her pet needed professional counseling. What the counselor learned was that this woman's daughter had died six months before her dog, and that the animal and her daughter had a close relationship together in the past. The woman felt like the dog was her last "tie" to her daughter, and so when he died, the woman fell to pieces.

In another case, a child became terribly upset weeks after a pet's death, and her parents consulted a mental-health professional for assistance. The parents themselves had not been seriously grief-stricken by their dog's death, and they had assumed that their child felt the same way. They then learned to their horror that the child had gotten the idea that if her parents didn't much care when the dog died, they probably wouldn't really care if she died too.

Upon discovering this, the parents assured her that they loved her very deeply and that they would be devastated if she died. The child was able to work through her grief with the assistance of the counselor and her parents. The girl and her parents also learned about the profound and complex aspects of grief and how it can affect people very differently.

In the next chapter, you'll learn some suggestions on how people can more effectively deal with their grief.

Chapter 4

Coping With Your Grief

The ancient Egyptians showed their grief at the loss of a family cat by shaving off their eyebrows. And if it was a dog that died, they shaved their entire bodies! They also rubbed mud in their hair to openly reveal to others their feelings of bereavement. Maybe the Egyptians had the right idea in overtly acknowledging the sadness that accompanies the loss of a beloved animal. You don't have to go quite so far with your own expression of grief, but one thing you do need to *do* is to acknowledge your grief to yourself and to also accept that it is a valid emotion. This chapter offers suggestions for you and other family members on making it through the grieving period.

Also keep in mind that there are some special times of the year when losing your pet can be especially traumatic; for example, during holiday seasons when everybody is supposed to be happy and when you may feel "wrong" for feeling so sad. There are also instances when you may think that the major portion of the grief is gone, but it all comes back to you in a flood of emotion on special occasions, such as on your pet's birthday or even on your own birthday. These issues are covered in this chapter.

Challenge Your Own Negative Thoughts

If you find yourself ruminating over thoughts which are making you feel depressed or very upset, one way to help yourself is to identify those thoughts which are negative and hurtful and then challenge them. The goal is to replace the negative and irrational thoughts with more positive and reasoned thoughts. It's called cognitive-behavioral therapy (CBT). It's a fancy name, although t it is not magic. Yet CBT can work effectively for many people. However, if you find that you can't effectively challenge your own negative self-talk and you are still severely bereaved and/or you are feeling stuck in your grief, then seek out the help of a therapist.

Challenging Negative Self-Talk

To use CBT at its simplest level, pay attention to the recurrent thoughts that are the most distressing for you. People constantly think different self-evaluating thoughts to themselves in their mind, and this is often referred to as "self-talk." All day long, you evaluate your own behavior as well as give yourself mundane instructions, such as, "Get bread on the way home from work." Pay attention to the thoughts that you are thinking and you may be surprised by how much is going on in your brain.

When you are grieving, if you keep thinking in your mind, "It's my fault that she died," then the next time that you "hear" that thought in your mind, work on challenging it as well as with replacing it with another thought. An example of a better replacement thought is: "I never wanted my pet to die. What happened was not intentional."

Table 4.1 offers some examples of negative and more positive self-talk for you to consider so that you may get the idea. Tailor these ideas to your own personal situation. Every time the negative thought comes up, challenge it and also replace it with the more positive thought. Eventually, the positive thinking will begin to dominate, at least on this issue.

Table 4.1: Negative Self-Talk and More Positive Self-Talk

Negative Self-Talk	More Positive Self-Talk
It's my fault that my pet died.	I never wanted my pet to die. What happened was not intentional.
I'll never forgive myself for letting her die.	My pet loved me. She would want me to forgive myself.
I don't know how I can go on without my pet.	It's very hard to lose a pet. After awhile, the pain will become more bearable.
No animal can ever replace my pet.	I'm not ready for a new pet now. I may be ready for one later.
I should have done more to help him.	I did my best and that is all anyone can do.
I should have noticed that he was taking much shorter walks. That must have been a sign he was really sick!	The vet said that there were no symptoms until he became very sick, and by then it was too late.

Thought Blocking

Another technique that may work for you, especially if you are having very depressed or distressed thoughts, is to use thought blocking. That is, the next time the very negative thought comes to your mind, such as "If only I had been home, Ruffy would not have died," here's what you should do. Imagine yourself saying loudly in your mind "Stop!" Every time that particular thought comes into your mind unbidden, say "Stop" in your mind again. Eventually, the thought should go away. Of course, continue to allow yourself to grieve and to think about the time you spent with your pet. Thought blocking should not be used as a means to avoid the normal grieving process.

If these or other suggestions in this book do not help you manage severe grief, it's important to seek help from a mental health professional. I also offer some suggestions of questions to ask a mental health professional before you sign up for therapy and they are provided in the next section.

Questions To Ask A Mental Health Professional

If you decide that you do need help from a psychologist, psychiatrist, social worker or another mental health professional, before seeing him or her in a professional relationship, I recommend asking the therapist the following questions first, to try to make sure that your therapist is likely to understand your grief about losing your pet. If the therapist answers "no" to most or all of these questions, then you should find another therapist, one who is more understanding of your problem.

1. Do you have a pet or have you recently had a pet?
2. Have you ever lost a pet to death?
3. If your pet died, were you upset about it?
4. Do you think it's normal to grieve when a pet dies?
5. Do you think that pets can improve mental health?
6. Have you ever treated someone who was very upset because a pet died?

You can probably come up with your own questions as well or replace these questions with ones that you word yourself. The point is that you want a therapist who can understand your grief, even when it's severe, and who doesn't think that it's very odd or bizarre to mourn the loss of an animal companion.

Some Do's And Don'ts

Based on the experiences of others who have mourned the loss of a companion animal, here are a few basic do's and don'ts that are related to your immediate pet loss.

- Do find someone to talk to about it
- Don't make major decisions while you're actively grieving
- Don't try to speed up the grief process
- Do change your routine
- Later, do visit places you and your pet went to together

- Do consider creating a special photo album
- Do consider a special site for burial

Do Find Someone To Talk To

Maybe the people you work with or your best friend thinks that you're being just plain silly to be so very sad over a pet's death. If so, then find someone who can understand your feelings, whether that person is a friend in your circle, someone on a pet support website, someone at the other end of a pet bereavement hotline, someone in a local pet grief support group, or elsewhere. (Ask your vet if she knows about any local groups.) Seek and you shall find someone. As mentioned, sometimes therapy may be needed, usually on a short-term basis of months. (The days when people saw therapists for years are long gone.)

Don't Make Any Major Decisions

When you are upset about your pet's death, it is not a good time to quit your job, tell your spouse that you want a divorce, move across the country to another city, or make any other major life changes. Give yourself a chance to grieve for at least a few months before making any major decisions about your life, because impulsive decisions that were made under stress may be poor choices for you.

Don't Try To Speed Up The Grief Process

Your grief may last a few weeks or months or as long as a year or more. (It should eventually subside from the extreme intensity of the grief that you feel immediately after the death of your pet.)

But it's important to realize that you can't rush through the grief process, just because you don't like it or you don't feel that it is productive. It's no fun, but you can't go around this lake of despair to resolve your grief. Instead, you have to slog through it. The problem with grieving is if you don't allow yourself to go through it now, then when you suffer from another loss later in life, that loss may be greatly intensified because you haven't recovered from the loss of your pet. So give yourself a break, and realize that grieving cannot be put on a timetable.

Surviving Your Pet's Death

Do Change Your Routine

Very often you will have created patterns associated with your pet; for example, you always walked your dog right after work or you played with your rabbit at a certain time of day.

If the pattern was a routine one between you and your pet, then it's a good idea to substitute another activity. Rather than sit and suffer over what you cannot do anymore because your pet is gone, do something else. Read a book, go to a park or call a friend. You may also wish to start changes of your routine before your animal companion dies if you know that he or she is terminally ill, in an attempt to prepare yourself.

After your animal's death, you may still wish to take walks as you did before with your animal, but consider taking them at a different time than your usual time or choose an alternative route. Changing the time pattern and/or the location of your walks can contribute to the healing process. It's not that you're denying your grief; instead you're creating ways to resolve it.

Later On, Do Visit Places You And Your Pet Went To Together

After telling you to change your walking patterns after your pet's death, it may sound contradictory to advise you to visit some of the special places where you went together with your pet. Yet after the immediate and severe grief subsides somewhat, and although it may also make you sad, visiting sites that you and your pet enjoyed together in the past can help alleviate the pain. For example, if you had visited the park together or enjoyed a dog-friendly beach, then you can go to the park or beach and remember your happy past times. This is different from what you did routinely with your animal, because these special sites were not part of your everyday routines.

Do Consider Creating A Photo Album

You may be able to gather pictures of your pet into a photograph album. The act of creating it as well as the opportunity to look at it later on can help ease your grieving. Cal said creating an album of all his photographs of Buttons, his much-loved cat, really helped him.

28

"That was the best therapy for me and it gave me something I'll have for the rest of my life. It solidifies my memories of him and puts those memories in one specific place," said Cal.

Do Consider Seeking A Special Site For Burial

Finding a place to bury your pet may be a healing experience for you, whether you choose a pet cemetery or your own backyard—assuming local regulations allow pet burial in your backyard. Or maybe you wish to have your pet cremated and you will keep the cremains in a special place.

Deciding on appropriate memorials or markers can also help. (See Chapter 8 for a further discussion on caring for your pet's remains.)

Other Options To Consider

Some other activities are worth considering because they may help you with dealing with your loss, including praying or considering religious verses or using art, music or journal-keeping to help you.

You May Find Solace In Religion

You may be among the people who find comfort and solace during your grief by turning to your religious faith. For example, Ronnie said it helped him with his grieving for Louis, his parakeet, to remember the Scripture verse about God knowing even when a sparrow falls.

Of course, some people have stated that their religion caused them problems when their pet died, because they had been instructed as children that animals could not go to heaven since they had no souls. Most animal lovers really cannot accept such a premise. (This subject is covered in the section "Do Animals Go to Heaven?" in Chapter 8 on helping children with their grief.)

Tammy assumed that her much-loved cat *would* go to heaven, and after talking it over with a friend, she decided to commend the soul of her cat to her deceased sister. This thought gave her a great deal of comfort. It might work for you as well.

Sometimes Music, Art, Or Journal Keeping Can Help

Listening to their favorite music helps some people with their grieving. Other people find it helpful to keep a journal of their feelings. You may also wish to paint or draw a picture of your companion animal.

Writing a poem or article about the animal can be a great creative and emotional release for many people. The ancient Greeks were very attached to their pets and often wrote poems about them after their deaths. Reading a poem or article may help you too. The "Rainbow Bridge" at the beginning of this book is a healing poem, and person after person has told me that it helped them with their grief.

Donating Money Or Services To Animal Charities

Other animal lovers find it helpful to send a check in the animal's name to the local animal shelter or to an animal charity. You may wish to do volunteer work at your local humane society or animal shelter. You may also choose to care temporarily for an animal who needs special care before entering a family permanently, as a "foster" parent to an animal.

Elaine donated a check to the local humane society in memory of her beloved collie Suzette and she received a letter from the director asking her if she would mind writing a tribute to her dog. Elaine was pleased to write a short article and this act also helped her to work through her grief.

Keeping Mementos Of Your Pet

Sometimes the grieving process can be helped by viewing items that your pet once played with or used. So don't immediately discard every one of your animal's items. One would think that keeping them would make you feel worse—but pet caretakers say that it actually gives them comfort.

When Marlene's dog Hoover died, she created her own memorial at home, framing a sympathy card that a friend had sent and gluing Hoover's tag on the corner of the card. She hung the card in the kitchen and says she looks at it often.

She also said that although she disposed of most of the "doggy things," she still kept the dog's harness and found herself pulling it out and smelling it for the first few days after the dog was gone. "I found it useful to keep one thing that smelled like him," she says.

An Exercise For You To Perform

Because many people blame themselves for their pet's deaths, even sometimes making wild leaps of logic in order to self-blame, please consider performing the following exercise if this situation applies to you. In fact, even if it doesn't apply to you, the exercise may help you with your grief. So read these brief instructions and try it out.

Get a piece of paper (or make a computer file), and at the top, list "Things I Did Right for My Pet." Then list everything you can think of that you did that showed your love for your pet. You are not allowed to list anything negative or any lapses in judgment that you may have exhibited in the past. Instead, only list what you did that was *right*. Your goal should be to list at least five or six items.

Everyone's list will be different. Here's my list for my dog Missy:

1. I took her for daily walks.
2. When Missy shook with fear during thunderstorms, I comforted her and hugged her and told her everything would be all right.
3. I tried to keep her away from our cats (who never liked her), so she wouldn't get scratched.
4. I put in the ear medicine when she had infections and cleaned out her yucky ears.
5. I told her frequently that she was a good dog. (And she was.)
6. I loved her a lot and she knew it.

After creating your list, read it over to yourself. If you're alone, read it aloud. Then put the list away, and the next time you start blaming yourself or feeling bad about the loss of your pet, read the list again.

How Do You Know If You Are Recovering From Your Grief?

Therapists often know when a client begins to recover from grief because of new behavior that the client exhibits. Donna Podrazik and her colleagues discuss some indicators of improved emotional health after clients received therapy for pet bereavement, describing these indicators in their 2000 article for the *Journal of Personal and Interpersonal Loss*. I have listed their key indicators of recovery in this section.

- You look happier to others. Rather than constantly looking sad or angry, you can sometimes smile or appear to be at peace.
- You re-engage in activities that you enjoyed prior to the death of the pet. Maybe before your cat became sick, you enjoyed gardening or swimming, activities that you abandoned when your beloved companion animal became ill and then died. When you start to resume these past fun activities, this is an indicator of improved emotional health.
- You no longer feel guilt for having days or experiences that are happy. While in active bereavement, you may feel like you will never be happy again. Then if something *does* make you happy, you become guilt-stricken because you thought you weren't supposed to be happy ever because of your pet's death.
- You form new relationships with other people. While actively grieving a deceased pet, it is hard to be interested in meeting new people. If you are now saying "yes" to making new friends, this is a positive sign.
- You are able to think of happy thoughts of your pet and not just about the death. For example, you think about the past and romping with the pet at the park or the funny or silly things that the pet used to do.

Helping Family Members

How can you assist other members of your household to deal with your pet's death? Begin with self-acceptance of your own emotions and extend that acceptance outward.

Want specifics? One tactic is to have a family meeting and have each person talk about how they miss the pet. If anyone brings up negative memories of the pet, don't chastise that person. Let him or her speak. An animal—or a person—is not sainted by dying and we all have good and bad memories of those we love.

You could also look at photographs of the pet together and talk about special times you had together. You may wish to create a scrapbook and/or pull out and frame a favorite photograph of your pet.

If you or someone in your family is computer-savvy, you may wish to scan old photos or even movies of your pet and then place them on an electronic picture frame. This picture frame will scroll through your photos or movies. This type of picture frame can be purchased at many stores or online.

Another common, and positive and healing reaction for families is to link the pet with special times that occurred in their lives and even with the whole tapestry of their lives, and to talk about those times together.

For example, Laurie said, "We got Brownie when Susie was two years old, and now Susie is sixteen!" Laurie recalls the time the family moved to the new home, and Brownie was so confused and excited.

How Long Does Pet Grief Last?

Because people vary so much in their attachments to their companion animals and also in their own individual circumstances (for example, how many previous losses that they've experienced, what's going on with their life right now, and so forth), it's really difficult to put a time limit on grieving. Some people may recover in a few months and others need more time.

Experts recommend that you give yourself up to about a year to grieve. There's a good reason for giving yourself a minimum of this one-year timetable. After a few months you may feel like you have pretty much recovered. But over the course of a year, different events that you link with your past and your animal companion will recur—but this time without the animal.

For example, let's say that you went camping with your dog every summer and the dog died in December. You were very sad, and then you thought you were "over" the grief. Then summertime comes around again, and you go out on a camping trip and you feel depressed and emotionally shaky. This grief may come flooding back because you're involved in an activity that you and your companion animal enjoyed together. The grief may come back for a few days or a week and it may be intense. It doesn't mean there's anything wrong with you—it's the normal grief process at work. Next year at this time you may again remember what it felt like to share activities with your pet—but as time passes, the good memories become stronger.

Different events may cause your grief to surge right back. For example, if you and your family celebrated your pet's birthday, as many pet caretakers do, you may feel very sad when that time comes around again. You may also feel sad on your own birthday, because you have been deprived of the companionship of the animal you loved.

At those times, you may wish to say a special prayer for your pet, if this practice fits in with your religious beliefs. Or just remember the joy that you shared with the pet.

Another circumstance that can renew the grief is if you see a pet that looks just like yours. You may irrationally (and momentarily) believe that a lady walking her dog that's the same breed as yours has kidnapped your dog —even though you saw your pet being euthanized. This is a natural, albeit irrational, reaction and you should not worry that you are losing your sanity if it happens to you.

Pet Grief Support Groups

Because so many pet lovers feel emotionally disenfranchised in not being allowed to grieve for their pets, sometimes a pet grief support group or pet bereavement group can offer you valuable help. Such a group is generally composed of volunteers and you may attend the group once or twice or become an active and regular member for months or longer. If your veterinarian doesn't know of any local groups, you should be able to find a website online to help you.

You may also wish to contact the nearest veterinary school in or near your state and find out if they have a helpful hotline phone number to provide you with help. Several hotlines for bereaved pet owners that are provided by universities are listed in Appendix B at the end of this book.

Do remember, however, than if you go online, it's best to use your first name only in chatrooms or other groups (or even to use a made-up name), to avoid individuals who may try to sell you items you don't need or take advantage of your grief in other ways.

Losing Your Pet Over The Holiday Season

It can be especially painful when your pet dies around Christmas or Hanukkah. Maybe the pet was a gift to you. Or maybe you just found it very difficult to join in the celebration when you are so sad over your loss.

The holidays can become stressful in and of themselves, what with people's high expectations, the family visits, and all the extra work. In fact, the holidays are often very disappointing, even without the death of a pet, and some people are greatly saddened by this.

Helen recalls the importance of her mixed-breed dog Krissy during Christmas: Her dog always sat on the sofa and watched the children open their presents.

When Krissy died at the age of twelve, Helen found it too difficult to celebrate Christmas in the same room, so she changed the location of the Christmas tree and gifts.

Realize that trying not to think about your grief by immersing yourself in holiday planning generally doesn't work. For this reason, even if it's "your turn" to plan dinner for twenty-eight relatives, if you feel that you can't handle it, then don't do it. Just say no.

And don't accept any "guilt trips" that relatives will probably lay at your door-step. You are entitled to your grief. When you are recovered next year, you can again become an active participant in the holiday whirls.

The next few chapters discuss some different types of circumstances in which pets die and the particular kinds of grieving associated with them. For example, Chapter 5 covers feelings that may occur when a pet dies suddenly, while Chapter 6 describes feelings that can happen to you when a pet dies after a long illness.

Chapter 5

When Your Pet Dies Suddenly

The deep sadness that you feel when a pet becomes suddenly ill and dies or is killed in an accident can be more severe than the grief that you feel when your pet has a long illness. Scientists have documented the greater intensity of grief felt by the owner of a companion animal who dies suddenly. The self-blame may be much greater as well.

Bob felt extremely guilty after his collie Max ran off and was killed in a car accident. Max had slipped his lead, and Bob rushed off to find him. The dog had been hit by a city bus. "I saw his body in the street and a few neighbors around him," said Bob. "1 leaped from the car—forget about 'park'—the car went off and bumped into a tree—and I lay down with Max. It was obvious he was dead. Someone loaned me a sheet and we wrapped him up and I took him home."

In another case described by researcher Froma Walsh in her 2009 article in *Family Process*, a husband had accidentally left the couple's terrier dog in the garage all day and the dog died. The husband tried to minimize his own guilt by telling his wife that they could go out and buy a new dog right away. This made the wife very angry because she felt like the husband didn't appreciate her deep attachment to the dog. She was also angry that her husband didn't accept his responsibility for the dog's death.

Feelings That Can Occur With A Sudden Death Of Your Pet

A sudden death can be very tough to handle. In contrast, the person who knows his or her pet is ill with a chronic and debilitating disease has had some chance to work through part of the grief before the pet's death. But when the pet dies quickly, the caretaker is often prone to ruminating over questions, such as why did she leave the door open—allowing the dog to run out and be run over by a truck? Or why didn't he notice that the rabbit looked sick that morning. (Perhaps the rabbit did *not* look sick in the morning—sometimes an illness can progress very rapidly and fatally.)

After the initial shock comes the reaction of alarm, with all the accompanying physical responses—rapid heartbeat, sweating, dry mouth, and others. If your pet was not yet an adult, the guilt and pain can be magnified, as you think of the life that this animal could have had—and was deprived of. And you may also think about the companionship you might have had. If, on the other hand, your pet has been a family member for a long time, you can scarcely believe that this has happened to you.

These powerful responses make it difficult for the grief-stricken person to maintain the normal routine of life.

Examples Of Sudden Deaths

Amy was particularly distraught over a freak accident that happened to her pet dove Amelia. The dove had lost a toenail and bled to death while Amy frantically fought to save her. She was full of guilt, albeit unwarranted, since she had done everything that she could. "The death occurred in about twenty-five minutes, with obviously little warning. I think the shock is worse this way," she says. "I beat myself up for not thinking like a paramedic! In some ways, the death seemed so avoidable. But I tell myself that if quick thinking and medical skills came so easily, people wouldn't have to be trained to do it well."

By comforting herself that she could have done no more than she did, Amy has managed to deal successfully with her grief, although her initial reaction was to cry and wail. "The grieving immediately thereafter was so intense that I thought that I would need to be sedated to ever sleep again," she says. "I think it must be particularly hard when you are trying to save your friend's life and you can't."

Sandy lost her cat Mimi in a very strange way. On the night that her younger daughter was born, Grandma was at Sandy's house babysitting the older children. Sandy says, "Our cat somehow got her collar caught on the heat-vent knob and she strangled to death right in front of my mother-in-law." The grandmother froze up and was unable to do anything. Thus, the joy over a new baby was dampened by the sadness over the death of a beloved pet.

Emma's cat Luigi died of hepatitis a week after he was diagnosed with the disease. She says, "It was the hardest thing I've ever had to deal with. I've had pets all my life, but this one was my all-time favorite. There was a rapport that just didn't exist with my other animals, even though I loved them too."

Luigi was in the hospital over the Labor Day Weekend and he died on Labor Day itself. "They wouldn't let us come in then [because it was a holiday], so there was a lot of guilt and concern that Luigi might have realized that we'd missed a day of seeing him," says Emma. "One of my biggest worries was that my cat didn't know that he was loved when he died. I kept dwelling on how terrible it must have been for him to be alone and in pain in an unfamiliar place."

Emma was able to resolve her grief, and says, "It was only in the process of helping someone else with similar feelings that I realized that everything my cat was in his life was confident and exuberant—he was the type of animal who could win over even the staunchest cat hater—and did. So it was a disservice to him to wonder if he doubted my love when he died."

She concludes, "The most important thing to keep reminding yourself is that it really does get better. Those first few months when it seems like there's no improvement are very difficult."

Sometimes animals rush off to investigate something outside that intrigues them, and a tragedy occurs—they are hit by a moving vehicle. Often you must deal with your own grief and pain and, at the same time you may be chastised by others for not controlling your animal better.

I can still remember the terror 1 felt when I was twelve years old and my dog Butchie ran into the street and was hit with a glancing blow by a bus. We rushed him to the veterinarian, who cleaned him up and said that he would need months of recuperation. We put him on the back porch in our kiddie swimming pool and my parents nursed him from there. Butchie made a complete recovery.

But others are not as fortunate as I was. Their animals are killed instantly or they die soon after an accident. Jay described his horror when, in response to his whistle, his two-year-old German shepherd, Rex, darted out into the street in order to reach him fast. Said Jay, "He was trying to show me what a good dog he was by rushing out." The dog was hit by a car and hurt very badly.

Jay comforted Rex, and then rushed him to the vet's office. The dog's breathing became ragged and strained, and it was clear that he was in respiratory distress. Rex stopped breathing and Jay pulled over and gave the dog CPR. It seemed to help, but then Rex shuddered and gasped and it became quite clear that he was dying. Jay remembers screaming the dog's name, as if he could bring his companion animal back to life if he yelled loudly enough. The vet confirmed that Rex was dead and reassured Jay that there was nothing more that he could have done.

Jay never had a chance to "make up" with his dog and to ensure that Rex knew he was loved. Or so Jay thinks. Yet I believe that Rex knew that he was loved. Not too many people will give mouth-to-mouth resuscitation to an animal and show as much caring and love as Jay did.

Another thing that was very hard for Jay occurred when he returned home. It was wintertime, and as he looked out the window, he saw Rex's tracks in the snow, going away from the house. But there were no paw prints coming back. "The snow didn't go away for two weeks and I had to look at those tracks every day," Jay sadly recalls.

Jim, a bird lover who devoted one room in his home to the care of his seven birds, suddenly discovered one day that his parakeet Webster had died. He describes it this way, "When 1 went into the bird room, there was a feeling like something was wrong. I checked on each of the birds to see if they were all right, and then noticed that Webster was not around. I then looked carefully and found him." Webster had died.

Jim says that he and his wife both experienced strong feelings of guilt over the death. "We were unable to spend more than about two minutes with our birds in each of the two days prior to his death, and that is unusual for us," says Jim. "The hardest part for me is wondering, 'Did I do something wrong?' As a paramedic myself, I think I've learned to deal with death. But I suspect old doubts came crawling to the surface when Webster died."

Paul considered his cat's Katrina death to be sudden, although the cat had been sick for about a month. "The hardest part was the fact that with all the technology that's available today, she had to get a disease that couldn't be cured and one that was past remission. And it was also hard to accept that there was absolutely nothing I could do to stop it, nor could I have prevented it."

Jim's anguish and self-blame and Paul's difficulty in accepting his cat's death are common reactions. But the fact is, we could watch our beloved animals day and night, and eventually they would die nonetheless. They are mortal, as we are.

If One Pet Attacks Another Pet

Katie told me that although there had been no previous signs of aggression, her cat Ditto was suddenly killed by one of her dogs, a wolfhound. "I was hysterical," she recalls. "It was so fast and it still haunts me. My first instinct was to kill the dog, and I did go get my revolver. But common sense prevented me from doing it."

It took quite a while for Katie to work through this grief, partly because of guilt and partly because of partially identifying with the animal's fear. "I felt so much guilt that I had inadvertently put him [the cat] in danger, and that I couldn't get to him in time. He had to be so confused and so terrified."

Through talking about the death with others and receiving the loving support of her family, Katie was able to resolve her distress, guilt, and pain. She says, "I should note that my mother and most of my friends have grieved with me for all of my pets that died, as did the neighborhood kids, who would come over to play with them frequently."

Sometimes you know that your companion animal is going to die, because your pet is suffering from a very serious or terminal illness. The next chapter covers key issues that are involved in this situation.

Chapter 6

When Your Pet Dies After A Long Illness

lthough it may not seem like much of an advantage when your pet is ill but is not in any imminent danger of death, in this situation you do have the chance to make a plan for his death and you also will probably have the opportunity to say goodbye. The type of grief you feel when your pet has had a long illness is unique to the person who has been caring for the pet for long-term and knows that now her companion animal is close to death.

Anticipatory Grief

Very often when you know that your pet is very sick or even terminally ill, the grieving starts before the pet's death. As the pet becomes sicker, your anxiety and grief levels increase. This is one way that your mind is attempting to prepare you for what lies ahead.

Use this time to think about the ceremonies and rituals that you may want to perform when your pet is gone, and to plan what you'd like to do with the remains of your animal companion. One family had professional photographs of their elderly dog taken with the family just before the animal was euthanized for a terminal illness. They found that this helped them tremendously with the coping process.

Caring For A Sick Animal Can Take Its Toll On You

Many interviewees have made great sacrifices of time and money in nursing a very sick animal. For example, Lucy is blind and her thirteen-year-old guide dog Rolf has himself gone blind. He is also incontinent, and has other serious health problems. But Lucy will not give him up and she is going to elaborate lengths to make him comfortable. For example, when she needs to go out, she takes her much younger guide dog with her and she also takes the older dog too. Lucy needs to realize that she can't cope with both her own needs and with the needs of Rolf. (See more on pet grief and disabled people in Chapter 10.)

Financial Costs May Be Steep

Providing care to a very sick animal can drain a person, physically and emotionally. And sometimes it can drain you financially as well. When Pete's snake Harold became very sick because his mother had accidentally overfed him, the vet said it would cost $2,000 to help the snake recover. Pete frantically called up all of his friends, and was able to borrow the money and Harold received the treatment. Unfortunately, Harold died soon thereafter from complications. Pete says he doesn't regret spending the money because it gave him more time with Harold, and the treatment *might* have worked. Of course, if you are in financial difficulties and $2,000 is a lot of money to you—as it is to most of us—you likely cannot afford to pay high bills.

Providing Care To A Sick Animal Can Be Draining

It's not just the cost of taking care of the animal but also the care itself that can be difficult. Administering injections and pills and perhaps even carrying the animal about everywhere can be a tough experience for anyone. Mandy's dog ChiChi was diagnosed with diabetes, and the dog needed several insulin shots every day in order to survive. But ChiChi didn't understand that the injections were keeping her alive, and she tried to bite Mandy every time, sometimes succeeding. Maybe your pet will pull through a serious illness. And maybe not. You have to rely on the advice of your veterinarian as well as your own gut-level feelings. Be sure to eat and sleep as much as you need to and don't neglect yourself. Remember that you won't be able to care for your animal if you should become ill yourself.

Relief And Sorrow

Sometimes after the animal succumbs to death or is euthanized, the caretaker can feel both relief and sorrow at the same time—relief because the animal is now beyond pain, and because the difficult and intense caregiving is at an end. But the caregiver then may feel guilty about her feelings of relief. Yet it is a normal human emotion to feel relief at the end of a difficult and painful experience and it in no way means that you are being disloyal to your pet.

Talk to empathetic friends and relatives too. If they've gone through the same thing, they may be able to provide you with good emotional support.

Planning Ahead Is A Good Idea — Even If Your Pet Isn't Sick Now

It's also a good idea to think about how you'd like to honor your pet after death, even if your pet isn't sick or elderly now. And if your pet is sick and/or elderly, it is very important for you to do so.

Yet many pet owners avoid this subject. They don't like to think about death and other "unpleasantnesses." Also, many pet owners are at least a little superstitious— thinking that if you plan ahead for your animal's death, then that will somehow make your pet die. This is what psychologists call "magical thinking," and it has no basis in fact at all.

The problem is that if your pet does die suddenly, it is very difficult to come up with a good plan fast. Many pet owners are too distraught, so they may leave the decision up to the veterinarian. A week or two later, they may wish that they had not agreed to cremation, for example, and instead wish they had buried the animal in a local pet cemetery. (See a listing of pet cemeteries in Appendix C of this book.) For these reasons, planning ahead is a good idea.

Some older animal caretakers take an even further step, thinking beyond their own lives and planning for someone to care for their animals in the event of their own death or disability.

Sometimes you will choose euthanasia for your pet so that your animal need not suffer a lingering and painful death. The next chapter covers key issues involved in making this decision.

Chapter 7

When Euthanasia Is The Choice: Dealing With This Pain

Just as humans sometimes succumb suddenly to a fatal ailment, so can pets, and sometimes the one best answer is choosing death for your pet rather than continuing to let him suffer. Greta left her two cats at a kennel over the course of a two week vacation, and she came back to see her "rather fat" cat Nietzsche transformed into a "bag of bones." The vet said the cat was very ill. Greta took the cat home and pampered her as much as possible, but the animal rapidly became weaker and weaker. Greta took the cat back to the vet, who said he was sorry, but Nietzsche was not going to recover. There was nothing more that could be done for her. Greta chose euthanasia for Nietzsche, because the cat was in so much terrible pain.

Watching your pet become more and more ill can be very hard, but veterinarians say that if your pet can still get around and obtain some enjoyment from life, there are many reasons (in addition to the fact that you love your pet!) for allowing him to die from natural causes rather than euthanasia. On the other hand, your pet may require more care than you could begin to provide. Or you may fear to see your beloved pet sinking deeper into even more severe pain. Euthanasia is a tough choice to make for any animal lover, especially when it is your beloved pet who is suffering.

Do know that just as there are people who criticize those who choose euthanasia (from the Greek words eu meaning "good," and thanatos, meaning "death"),
you may also face critics who think that you should use euthanasia. Remember,
you are the one who has to make this choice for yourself and your pet and the main
goal is not to make other people happy or impressed but instead, to do what you
think is best for your animal companion.

Making The Choice

The decision for or against euthanasia is a difficult one, but often your veterinarian
can help you with information and advice. There are also stages that you may go
through in making your decision, described in this section.

Talk To Your Veterinarian

Talk with your veterinarian about the euthanasia choice. Also remember that
your veterinarian is an animal lover. So if you do choose euthanasia, while you
are sobbing about your pet's impending death, the vet is the one who will be
causing the death and this can be very emotionally draining for her. She needs to
have worked out that issue in her mind. Thus, even though she's a professional,
don't be surprised if the vet is also upset or distressed.

Your veterinarian can be a great help on this issue, discussing with you the
probability that your pet might get better, and advising you of the degree of pain
that your animal feels.

In addition, the vet may be able to help you come to terms with the fact that
euthanasia is often a compassionate act, rather than an aggressive or negative one.

Stages of Decision Making in Euthanasia

In a chapter in *Pet Loss and Human Bereavement*, a book that is oriented to
veterinarians, authors Leo K. Bustad and Linda M. Hines identify six stages/
reactions that are related to a pet owner's decision about euthanasia.

Frustration and ambivalence. In this stage, the human companion doesn't want
the pet to suffer. But at the same time, he doesn't want to lose the animal to death.
These mixed feelings can cause considerable tension.

Acknowledgment of suffering. Now the human companion accepts that the pet is
truly suffering and decides to allow the animal to be euthanized by the veterinarian. The decision is made, but emotions still run very high at this point.

Anger. In this stage, children may blame their parents for the death of the animal or spouses may blame each other. Or everyone may decide to blame the veterinarian. None of these reactions is "fair"—but despite this, they are very common reactions.

Loss. In this stage, the common grief reactions of crying, sleeplessness and malaise may be evinced by the distressed pet lover.

Guilt. Another frequent reaction to the euthanizing of a pet is a very strong sense of guilt. Couldn't you have done just one more thing? Usually the vet provides reassurance at this point that the caretaker did indeed choose the right course of action for the sick animal.

Self-protection. A final stage that many people who euthanize their pets go through is the "self-protection" stage. This occurs when the owner decides that he or she will never acquire another pet because they believe that they could not bear to go through this much emotional pain again. They perceive this choice as protecting themselves. However, many animal lovers eventually do change their minds later on, deciding that they miss the love of a companion animal. (See Chapter 12 for more information on how to know if you're ready for a new pet.) Still, some people continue with the decision to remain petless through life.

Factors To Consider

Experts say one way to determine if euthanasia is the right choice for your animal companion is to think about the activities that you have enjoyed with the animal in the past or that he or she enjoyed alone.

The next thing to do is to ask yourself if your pet can still do some or even any of these favorite activities. And finally, ask yourself if you think that your pet is really happy. As a person who loves his pet, you don't want him to leave you and you don't want to be the one that causes him to leave you. Yet the important thing to do is to try hard to consider the best interests of the animal and his quality of life.

Sometimes The Animal "Lets You Know" When It's Time

Although it is very difficult to make the decision for euthanasia, some pet caretakers report that the animal may let you know in both overt or subtle ways when it's the right time to choose euthanasia.

"I had signs from Molly," said Sally, owner of a sixteen-year old poodle who had been diagnosed with cancer. "They were the kinds of signs that those who have known and loved and bonded with an animal can understand—that she was ready to let go. I had wanted to give her a high-quality life for as long as possible, and then to let her go peacefully, without any suffering." And so she did.

Said Tina, a grieving caretaker of a beloved boxer, "I was so worried that I wouldn't know when it was time, but Merlin let me know—he had greeted me every day when I came home for eight years. But that Monday night, he didn't even try to meet me, he was so tired, sick and in obvious pain."

You may feel particularly upset if there are expensive procedures that might save your pet, but you just can't afford them. Experts say that this decision can be a complicating factor. But if you cannot afford costly surgery or other alternatives, it is not your fault. Veterinarians point out that the expensive procedures might not "work" anyway.

Should You Be There With Your Pet When Euthanizing Occurs?

Sometimes people wish to be with their animals when the euthanizing is done and sometimes they don't. Veterinarians say that if you feel that you will become too distraught or even hysterical, you will do your pet no good in her final moments. But how do you know how you will react? It's hard to predict, particularly if this is a new situation for you. One possible way is to envision the scene in your mind and imagine how you might react. It's also a good idea to rely on your gut-level emotions about whether or not you could handle being present during the procedure.

Others feel that it's important to be with the animal at the end, so that the animal will not be frightened or feel alone.

Polly found a middle ground to being present at the euthanasia; she placed her hands on her cat Muffin and closed her eyes as the euthanasia was performed. By doing so, she didn't have to actually watch the procedure, but her pet could feel comfort from her touch.

Lisa has had several pets euthanized, and she says that in some cases she was present and in some cases she was not there. "Last year, I lost a pet to cancer. There were treatments to try, but ultimately they all failed. I had read articles about being there with your pet at the end, and decided that no matter how painful it was to me, 1 wanted to be there in those final few moments."

She continues, "I called the vet to let her know it was time. I gathered Mimi's favorite blanket and found some catnip in the garden. I placed the blanket on the table and put Mimi on it." The vet explained to Lisa what would happen and everything happened just as she said it would. "Mimi slipped quietly away and ended her suffering," said Lisa.

Sometimes pet owners liken the experience to when a beloved human is ill, and they believe that with euthanasia they can help their pets more than they were able to help the humans they have loved. Tom said he lost his mother to cancer and he remembers that he could do nothing to help her, but could only helplessly watch her die in severe pain. "She wanted to die so bad," he said. But it is not legal to euthanize suffering humans.

On the day of her death, Tom saw his mother make a gesture that looked to him as if she were trying to smile. He asked her if that was what she was doing, and she nodded. He believes that she was smiling because she knew the end of her suffering was near. He later remembered this experience when his cat Suki became very ill. Tom knew that he could release his pet from the suffering that he couldn't save his mother from experiencing.

Having Other Pets Present During Euthanasia

Other animals in your household are often affected by the death of a pet, and they may cry, fail to eat, and act generally depressed. As a result, some caretakers believe it's a good idea to bring in your other pets when your companion animal is euthanized, if you can. For example, Lisa brought in her other cat who loved her sick cat when the euthanizing occurred. Some vets say that this can ease the problem of your other pets spending weeks looking for their lost friends. Ask your vet if this is possible.

Use common sense—if the euthanasia is to be performed in the vet's office, limit the number of other pets that you bring to one or two. And do be sure to get permission from the vet beforehand.

Amy took her other pet into the vet's office for the euthanizing, as previously arranged with him. "We have a nine-year-old cocker mix, Jolie. And when we had Pepper, our dalmation put down, Jolie was in the room." Any said that Jolie's behavior was very different from her usual actions. "Jolie usually would have been right in the middle of everything, wanting the attention for herself." But on this day, Jolie held back. "When it was over, I looked at Jolie, and she was watching, with the saddest eyes I have ever seen. I think she understood," said Amy.

After The Euthanasia — Sometimes Relief

Many people report relief when the euthanasia is over, just as some pet owners are relieved when their pet dies of natural causes after a long and debilitating illness. So much stress has been carried up to that moment. And the person may have spent weeks or months of intensive caregiving, watching the animal get sicker and sicker. The pet is now at peace.

And yet with the relief may come guilt. How can you be glad that your pet is dead? Are you a terrible person? Understand that feelings of relief are natural, and no, you are not a bad person if you experience this emotion.

Some Practical Considerations

If you do choose to euthanize your pet, make a late afternoon or evening appointment or an appointment at a time when the waiting room at the animal clinic will not be crowded. Then call ahead before you leave for the vet's office, to ensure that the vet hasn't suddenly become tied up with emergencies, and now has a waiting room of people.

One man said he specifically asked the veterinarian if he could enter and leave through the back entrance. "I didn't want to have to come through the front afterward because I was afraid I'd start bawling in front of everyone," he said. His veterinarian agreed.

Ask the vet if you can either prepay or be billed. You might feel especially bad about paying the bill right after the pet is euthanized.

Discuss with the vet how the pet's remains will be handled and whether you want the disposal of the remains. Tell the vet if you wish to choose cremation and/ or if you want your pet buried at a pet cemetery or are considering other options for his remains.

Get someone to go with you to the veterinarian's clinic. Even if the other person does not wish to witness the euthanasia, he or she may be able to drive you home afterwards if you are too upset to drive. This should be a person who is not as attached to your pet as you are, so that he or she will be emotionally able to provide you with any needed support.

Many times people receive great comfort from the ritual of burying their pets. The next chapter discusses the option of pet cemeteries and cremation, as well as the unique option of mummifying your pet.

Chapter 8

Caring For Your Pet After Death: Considering Options

Many bereaved pet owners find that a pet funeral or other memorial ritual greatly helps with the grieving process. Such a ceremony is a chance to acknowledge the love and importance of the pet in their lives. The oldest pet cemetery in the United States, established in 1896, is the Hartsdale Pet Cemetery. This cemetery is located in Hartsdale, New York. There are about 600 pet cemeteries nationwide in the United States and some of them are listed in Appendix C in this book.

You can create your own ritual or ceremony and your children can participate or you may receive help from a pet cemetery or memorial service in creating a ceremony. You may also find such a prospect too painful and prefer that a caring veterinarian take care of the remains for you, rather than using a pet cemetery. Others choose to have their pets' ashes strewn in a special place.

Burying Your Pet in the Backyard

Assuming that your pet is not large and there are no city ordinances against burying your pet in the backyard, this may be the right option for you. "We buried our parakeet below the window that he used to look out of and that the other birds still look out of," said Andy.

If you don't own your own home, but are renting a home or apartment, you don't have the legal right to bury your animal in the backyard. Ask the owner or landlord if you can do so—he or she may be an animal lover too, and may give you permission. If you own your own home, check with local authorities to ensure that you comply with any regulations that may exist.

In a poignant letter to his daughter, Barry described the frenzy in which he dug his dog Blue's grave, overcome with anguish at the loss he experienced.

"I had never dug so deeply before," he wrote, "and I was like a crazy man, working too fast, just a digging machine, feeling nothing. Down around a foot and a half deep, it started to get rocky and this meant not just shoveling. Just getting the rocks out, I broke the shovel we've had for fifteen years. Then I started to claw the rocks out with little gardening tools and my bare hands. When I was satisfied it was deep enough, though it wasn't really a warm night, I was sweating profusely and it wasn't all from the effort."

John recalls when his two sons, then ages fourteen and fifteen, were worried about their cat Beulah. Beulah was thirteen and had been in their family since the boys were toddlers. She was missing and so they went in search of her and found her. She had died.

Both boys were very upset, although they tried to put brave faces on, and they insisted on conducting a funeral. Says John, "They wrapped the body in cloth, dug a grave in the backyard, took a boom box out and played funeral music, and had a memorial service. They then buried the cat, put a rock marker on the grave, and came back inside."

Choosing To Cremate Your Pet

Increasing numbers of people are deciding on cremation to manage the remains of their beloved animal companions. They may reason that cremation is what they plan for themselves when they die, and so they also consider it a good alternative for their pets. They may also see it as an "environmentally friendly" choice because cremation will destroy any bacteria or disease that is left in the animal after death, and thus will not contaminate the area.

You may choose either a mass cremation, in which your animal will be cremated at the same time as other animals, or an individual cremation, in which case your animal would be cremated alone and you could then have access to the cremains (the ashes), either for keeping or for burial. Check with your veterinarian to make sure both these options are available.

You may choose to bury your pets' cremains on your own property (if this is legal) or in another special place. "We had Pepper cremated and we still have her ashes," said Amy of her thirteen-year-old dalmatian. She had a unique approach to the dispersion of the cremains.

"We are going to bury some of the ashes here at our house, under the apple tree and among the poppies, and we'll plant her a red primrose. Another part we will take to our favorite camping spot and scatter them there. And the third part we are saving until we move to the home where we plan to live in until we retire."

When Jenny's dogs—Pepsie, a fourteen-year-old sheltie, Lassie, an eighteen-year-old sheltie, and Napoleon, a fifteen-year-old beagle—died at different times, she had each dog cremated. Jenny then had the cremains and the dog collars for each dog sewn into pillows with the dog's name embroidered on the pillow. "These pillows with the ashes and collars will be put in my casket when I die and will be buried with me," Jenny said.

You may wish to keep your pet's remains in an urn or special container in your home and there are many attractive vessels available through pet cemeteries.

Pet Cemeteries: Pros And Cons

Before she died, wealthy Leona Helmsley stipulated in her will that upon her death, her beloved dog Trouble would be buried with her and her husband. However, she apparently did not realize that many state laws (and New York is one of them) prohibit burying pets with humans in human cemeteries. Interestingly, however, if Helmsley had been buried in a pet cemetery (which could have been arranged), then the pet could have spent his eternal rest with her, according to Stanley Brandes of the University of California at Berkeley in his 2009 article for *Ethnology*.

The key advantage of a pet cemetery is basically the same advantage as for a human cemetery: It provides a last resting place for a beloved companion, and it is also a place where you can visit periodically. (See a listing of some pet cemeteries in Appendix C at the end of this book.) Your veterinarian should know about pet cemeteries in your area. Most pet cemeteries concentrate on dogs, cats, and other relatively small animals, although some facilities may accept horses and large animals, charging a higher rate.

Often the staff at the pet cemetery handles funeral services as well. Some pet cemeteries operate in conjunction with other pet businesses (such as kennels and veterinary hospitals), while others are solely dedicated to the cremation and/or burial of pets.

Another advantage to a pet cemetery is that hopefully the cemetery will always be there. In contrast, if you've buried your pet on your land, you might someday move away. Military people have found pet cemeteries to be a good option for this reason.

There are also costs involved with a pet cemetery, such as the cost of the site where the pet will be laid to rest, the expense for the funeral service and the cost for memorials (markers) identifying that your pet was buried in this site. Memorials can be made of marble, granite, bronze, or other substances. Other costs may be involved as well. Note: You may be able to purchase memorials by mail, but do know that some pet cemeteries have certain specifications that must be met for markers. Check first with the pet cemetery before making your purchase.

You should also check on what would happen to the cemetery in the event that the owners died or retired. Is there a trust fund or some other provision to maintain the cemetery in that event? Although the management of many cemeteries provides for this contingency, don't take it for granted.

Some pet cemeteries offer the option of dedicating a tree, bench, garden, and so forth to the memory of your pet and will generally also provide a plaque.

What To Look For In A Pet Cemetery

When you're acutely grieving, it can be hard to evaluate a pet cemetery, so if possible, you should try to make arrangements for your pet beforehand. Whether you can make advance arrangements or not, consider the following guidelines:

- Is the pet cemetery clean and well kept? Does it look like people really care about the upkeep? Make a visit to the site and personally check it out.
- Are the people at the pet cemetery open, friendly, and helpful? Do they answer all your questions?
- Has the cemetery been there at least a few years, so it has a track record? It's not a good idea to sign up with a cemetery that opened last week.

- Is the land where the pet cemetery is situated owned by the proprietors or a corporation, and not leased or rented? Ask.
- Ask the owners or managers if they have any information or can recommend any readings on pet bereavement. If they are clueless as to what you are talking about, this is a bad sign.
- What provisions have they made for the future? This may be done in several ways; for example, it can be stated in the deed that the land is for the pet cemetery use only. Or it can be done by contract, and the contract between the pet owner and the cemetery should stipulate how long the area is guaranteed to remain a pet cemetery.
- Is the cemetery large enough? Experts say it should be at least five acres in size.

One Unique Option: Mummification Of Your Pet

Some pet owners choose other options. For example, the company Summum, which is located in Salt Lake City, Utah, offers the service of mummification of animal companions.

According to the company's website in 2012, the cost for the mummification process ranges from $4,000 for a pet that weighs up to 15 pounds to much higher rates. For example, the cost for mummifying an animal of 61-100 pounds is $28,000. Extra required costs are associated with placing the mummified animal inside the mummiform, the device in which the pet will be encased. For more information, go to their website at www.summum.org.

Many adults don't understand that children grieve for their pets, nor do they grasp how children grieve. The next chapter is devoted to helping children deal with this loss.

Chapter 9

Helping Children With Their Grief

C hildren can react very strongly to the loss of a pet, although not all children become visibly distressed and upset. How parents and other caring adults explain the death of the animal to children can help ease the child's pain or make it worse. But remember, you can't make the grief vanish quickly, as much as you really hate to see your child suffer. Children will grieve the death of a pet they loved—this is a given. Experts say that often a child's first experience with grief associated with death occurs after the death of a pet. Their ability to cope with this loss may well enable them to deal with future losses.

Avoid Making Common Mistakes

Many adults remember back to their childhood and how their parents handled (or mishandled) explaining to them the death of their pets. For example, some parents may have said that the animal ran away, when in fact—as the child later found out—the pet was accidentally killed or was euthanized. The running away explanation often leads to the child frantically (and fruitlessly) searching the neighborhood for the pet.

Wanda, now a grown woman, still hasn't forgiven her mother for her handling of the death of a pet. She said she actually saw her puppy get run over by a truck in front of the house—and her mother forced her to go to summer camp that day anyway, as previously planned. Wanda recalls that she was an emotional wreck that day and for the next few weeks.

Wanda's mother promised her a new dog upon her return from summer camp, despite the child's hysterical crying that she did not want another dog. And when she returned, sure enough, there was a new puppy waiting. Wanda was not allowed by her mother to talk about her love for the pet who had died. Instead, it was a sort of surrealistic experience because her mother pretended that it had never happened. Wanda's mother followed this pattern each time that a pet died, refusing to allow Wanda a chance to grieve or to even acknowledge that there was any grief.

"Of course 1 fell in love with the new pets pretty quickly once they showed up in my life," Wanda recalls. "But in looking back, I can see that this instant-replacement stuff took its toll, because I never really had the opportunity to grieve and work through that grief for any of my pets."

No One Perfect Way To Explain

Don't expect to do a perfect job in explaining the death of a pet. The primary thing to remember in explaining the pet's death to your child is to say that the animal has died, instead of saying the animal ran away, got sick at the veterinarian's office, or offering some other false explanation to your child. You need not provide any gruesome details if the death was a bad one, but do be truthful that the animal has died.

Two Common Mistakes

Parents make two primary mistakes in talking about the death of a companion animal with a child. One is in expecting the child to grieve in the same manner as an adult. Children should be acknowledged as individuals and as children whose reactions may be very different from yours.

The other common mistake is to fail to interpret the child's behavior as grief-related because the child may not cry or talk about the animal. For example, anger and acting out, even if the child says nothing about the animal that has died, may have a direct relationship to the child's grief reaction over the loss of their pet and may also be the means by which the child exhibits her distress.

Your Own Reactions To The Pet's Death

Keep in mind that your body language, voice, and overall demeanor will reveal to the child that something is wrong, even if you don't say what it is. Here's a helpful hint: Tell the child yourself about the death whenever possible before others impart details and (possibly) mishandle the telling and frighten your child.

An Example Of An Explanation That Almost Went Wrong

Bonnie spoke of what she did when her little daughter's turtle Henry disappeared and was "presumed dead." She rushed down to the pet store to try to find a turtle just like him so that she could pretend that nothing had happened at all. She wanted to spare her three-year-old child any pain. But none of the other turtles looked even remotely like Henry.

"I had just gotten divorced, and this was my first major single-parent trauma, so I very maturely began sobbing hopelessly in the pet store," she recalls. "The kindly old pet-store manager took me into his office and I explained the situation."

He convinced Bonnie that it was *not* a good idea to try to trick her child by replacing the turtle with a look-alike replacement, and advised her instead to allow the child to grieve and to obtain another pet when she and her child both felt ready. She followed this good advice.

Other Explanations

Judy found her parrot Shirley dead in the morning, and she thought carefully about how to explain the death to her five-year-old son. Judy prepared a little casket for Shirley and told her son Blake that the animal was dead. Judy and Blake dug a grave in the backyard, said prayers, buried Shirley, and put flowers on the grave.

Jerry recalls his parents' explanations of the death of a fish, bird, hamster, guinea pig, or cat. "They simply told us what happened. They explained that the animal was not in pain anymore." Jerry continues, "My parents told me that there was lots of room in heaven for animals because people loved them so much." He added, "I also remember my mom waking me up in the middle of the night to watch a litter of kittens be born. They wanted us to see life begin too."

Common Grief Reactions Of Children

Children who are grieving the death of a pet suffer from many of the same symptoms as bereaved adults: crying, headaches, stomachaches, and other reactions may occur at any age. Children may also isolate themselves from their friends and classmates and refuse to go to school. Some children exhibit hypochondriac symptoms.

In addition, a preschool-or elementary-school-aged child who has had problems with bedwetting in the past might find that problem recurring. Daydreaming may become prominent with grieving children of any age, as well as feelings of apathy, anxiety, and depression. The child's self-esteem may drop.

Sometimes children will act like they don't care about a pet's serious illness, and the reason for this is often that they are hoping that if they ignore it, then the problem will go away. This is a form of "magical thinking," and let's face it—many adults engage in it too.

Another reason for pretending not to care is that the child, particularly a male, may believe that it is unacceptable or unmasculine to grieve. This is a culturally ingrained belief. Don't expect your son to sob in front of you, but do tell him that full-grown men who loved their pets often do cry when a much-loved animal dies. Allow him the privacy to grieve alone.

Some childhood symptoms of grief at the loss of a pet may include:

- Apparent indifference or apathy
- Excessive clinginess
- School difficulties
- Constant daydreaming
- Fear
- Anxiety
- Acting out
- Nightmares
- Crying or sobbing
- Rumination (thinking over and over about the circumstances of the animal's death)
- Guilt
- Anger
- Moving in and out of grief
- Playacting the animal's death
- Drop in self-esteem

- Destructive behavior
- Reclusiveness or self-isolation

Will Your Kids Be Mad At You For Euthanizing The Pet?

It is possible that your children will be angry or resentful that you chose euthanization for your ill companion animal. And this is probably one of the main reasons (other than causing the child emotional pain) for people not telling the kids about the euthanasia. They don't want their children to hate them. But sometimes in doing the right thing, your children will be angry with you, whether it's that you euthanized a very sick pet or took another entirely unrelated action.

If the children are angry with you after the euthanizing, try to accept this as a natural reaction and it will generally pass. (They will be more angry if they find out that you lied to them.) Try to emphasize the positive experiences you and the children enjoyed with the animal. Explain that you wanted to release the animal from physical pain and you believed this was the only way. And allow them their anger and their grief.

Warning: Do not tell your child that the pet was "put to sleep" if your animal was euthanized or died in some other way, especially if the child is younger than an adolescent. Some children may then fear going to sleep, lest it lead to their deaths. In one case, a child needed a minor medical procedure and became hysterical when the doctor, in an attempt to reassure him, told him he was going to give him some medicine to "put him to sleep." It took a great deal of explaining before the child realized the doctor was not going to end his life.

Consider Your Child's Age In Explaining

How you tell your child about a pet's death should vary according to the age of the child, and a ten-year-old child can generally understand far more than your four-year-old. Don't presume, however, that your toddler doesn't notice the pet is gone. Parents have reported their small children searching the house repeatedly for a pet that is no longer there.

Preschool Children

Even infants and toddlers can react to an animal's death, sometimes because they are responding to your reactions. They may act out and be generally difficult. And you can't really explain what happened: they won't understand.

Preschool children may be unable to understand the finality of death and may repeatedly ask you when the pet will be "coming back." Don't worry that your four-year-old is "in denial." He likely cannot grasp the difficult concept of death.

It's also important to understand that often young children identify with the pet. This is why it's important to avoid saying that a pet died because it was sick. (See the list of do's and don'ts later in this chapter.)

Children of this age may act out funerals or burials, for example, burying their stuffed animals or dolls in the sandbox. Don't assume this behavior is morbid and rush the child off to a psychologist. Children explore subjects, sometimes very difficult ones like death, through play.

Children Ages 5 To 9

Children who are ages five and older are beginning to have a grasp of death, but they cannot fully understand its finality until after about age nine or ten. Instead, children in this age group continue to fantasize that death only happens to the very old and can generally be avoided. This is a common belief among children of this age and it's not a good idea to expend great efforts in order to convey the finality of death to the child. Developmentally, they will probably be unable to grasp what you're trying to convey and you may only frighten or confuse them.

Children of this age may also wish to discuss the animal's death with their friends and add many elaborate details to the story. This is normal behavior for children of this age.

Preadolescence And Adolescence

Preadolescent children begin to understand what death is, and they may be very frightened by it. You need to give them plenty of comfort and TLC. The child may suffer nightmares and appetite problems and a host of other symptoms. They may fear their own death and your death and will need reassurance. You can't tell them that they will never die or that you will never die, but you can reassure them that they and you are healthy and can expect to live for many years.

Adolescents are particularly vulnerable to suffering from grief. Yet they may be the least likely to show their grief because it's not "cool" or sophisticated to cry your eyes out about your rabbit dying. Don't press them hard to talk out their feelings, but do make it clear that it's okay to feel sad and that you are available to talk about the pet if they want to talk.

Be aware that how *you* think and feel about death may have no connection with how your child regards death. Be an active listener. Although it's a good idea to share anecdotes and say how you felt when you were his age and your pet died, it's also important to listen to the child's own words, observing his body language, and responding to and validating his feelings.

You may also tell the child that you are having trouble dealing with your own grief with this new death, but that you'll do your best to answer questions and help understand his feelings.

Because teenagers are not expected to be very "huggy" with their parents, and yet they still have a need for tactile comfort, the loss of a pet can be very painful for them. Some experts have said that pets also function as a transitional object to adulthood or a comfort object—somewhat similar to the blanket that the toddler must have when it goes to sleep.

As a result, experts say that adolescents may have a more difficult time than younger children in resolving their grief over a pet's death.

Reassure Children Of All Ages That It's Not Their Fault

Many adults blame themselves for the death of a pet, so it should not be surprising that children are also likely to think their animal died because of some action or inaction on their part. (Or your part.) Or they make think that the animal's death is a punishment from God or from fate for bad behavior. If only Billy hadn't hit Jimmy in school today, then the dog would not have died. Refute such illogical thinking and explain that one thing has nothing to do with the other.

Children need to be reassured that the cat didn't die because they didn't do their homework or they failed to take out the garbage. Or it's because they argued about feeding the cat or going with you to the veterinarian. Or because of negative thoughts they may have had about the animal. For example, such thoughts as, "Oh, why do I have to take this dumb dog for a walk. I wish I didn't have to!" And now they don't have to walk the dog anymore because the dog has died. So they got their "wish," and now feel guilty about it. But their thinking didn't make it happen, and this should be made clear to the child.

Allow The Children To Talk About The Pet

Because the death of a pet is a painful experience to acknowledge, it may seem easier to brush away a child's questions and concerns. But experts say it is far better to allow the child to talk about how he or she feels. In addition, you may wish to alert the child's teacher that a beloved animal has died so she will understand any changes in behavior or performance.

If you have photographs of the children with their pets, pull them out and let your children reminisce about the good (and even the sometimes annoying) behavior of their pets.

Listen to your child. Most people have two ears, and if they're both working, they may assume that they are a good listener. Wrong! Many people are not very good at listening. Here are some basic tips to help you listen to your child:

- Let the child finish talking before you rush in to make a comment. Adults are often very bad about interrupting children.
- Withhold judgment about what the child has said. Her feelings are valid even when you feel differently.
- Try to determine what the child's main feelings or concerns seem to be and summarize what she has said. For example, "It sounds like you are saying that you wish you could have told Brownie just one more time that you loved her. Is that right?" Listen to her response. If you got it wrong the first time, try again.
- Offer condolences. For example, tell the child that Brownie knew that she was loved. Provide examples, such as the many times that Brownie leaped into the child's lap when she arrived home from school.
- Validate the child's feelings. "It's hard to feel this sad."

Get Help From Others

You may be able to work with a member of the clergy in acknowledging the death of the pet as a significant loss. Your child's teacher has probably also dealt with this issue before and may have some recommendations for you. The teacher may also bring the subject up in class and allow a certain amount of healing and catharsis by recognizing the child's loss.

Children's books on pet loss can help too. Ask your children's librarian at the public library or the school librarian for assistance in identifying the best books to read to your child at her level of understanding.

Avoid Saying These Things To Children Younger Than Adolescents

There are common statements that many parents make to their children, possibly because their own parents made them to them. Sometimes these statements can cause more emotional turmoil and upset. Avoid the following:

- "Fido went on a long journey." It sounds nice, but children are very literal and you don't want them to think they are going to die if they go on a vacation with you.
- A similar error is to tell the child that "Kitty is on an eternal sleep." Again, don't make sleep equal death in the child's mind.
- "The cat ran away because he wasn't happy" is the wrong thing to say if what really happened was the cat died naturally or was euthanized. This explanation can also make the child feel rejected and abandoned—after all, why wasn't the pet happy? Was it the child's fault? The child will wonder, even if he or she doesn't verbalize this question.
- "We loved him so we had to let him go." This statement can be very frightening to a child. After all, you love him, so does that mean you could let him go? Or worse, make him die? These are certainly not ideas you want to convey to your child. Instead, emphasize that the pet was very old (if she was) and very sick or hurt (if she was).
- "God took him." Or "God took him because he was good." This may makes God sound very ominous, as if He could suddenly swoop down and take a person. Even if you believe this, such an idea is very threatening for a child. Also, if God took the pet because he was good, does this

mean you should be bad so that God won't take you? This is literal reasoning that many children use. Instead, if you are religious, it is better to say that the animal died and then (if you are comfortable with saying this) he went to heaven.

- "He passed on." To where? And why? This vague explanation only begs a lot of questions from children. Don't use it.

Don't Fear The "D-Word"

Experts say that parents are often afraid of using the word "death" because it sounds too frightening. They want to shelter their children, which is why they use phrases like "went to sleep" and so on. But our children do see death, on television and in real life. They see animals that were run over in the streets and they know that death happens. They may not fully understand it, and it's your job as a parent to try to explain death at your child's level of understanding.

Help Your Child Express Feelings

It may help a young child to draw a picture of the animal. Older children can write down their feelings or even write a poem or a tribute to the pet. (Adults find this to be very helpful too.) And be sure to tell your child, whatever his or her age, that sad feelings are normal for someone whose pet has died. Crying is normal. Feeling upset is normal. Explain that these very sad feelings will subside after a while, although the child may always remember the pet and the good times they shared.

Do Pets Go To Heaven?

Some children—and adults—worry over what happens to the animal's soul when it dies. That is, if you believe in heaven, can you be assured that your pet will meet you there? And do animals have souls? Although these questions may sound silly to some, to others they are of real concern.

Some theologians argue that animals can't go to heaven because they don't have souls. Each reader will have her own beliefs regarding life after death. But the idea of a pet going to heaven can be comforting to children and adults.

Barbara remembers that when she was about ten, a friend's dog died and she was terribly upset. At chapel that morning, the Episcopal priest was talking about animals. When one of the children asked him if animals go to heaven, he answered that if they didn't, then he didn't want to go there either. Barbara says, "Perhaps this was not theologically sound, but it made us all feel better, and for some reason, it has stuck with me all this time."

Mary continued to be bothered by whether animals go to heaven from her childhood and into adulthood. "The hardest thing for me about losing my animal companions has been getting past the nuns telling me that animals don't have souls and when they are dead, they are gone." She continues, "I no longer believe this and a sense of the continuity and connection of all things helps me deal with this grief."

Maybe animals DO have a soul. Larry swore that one night when he was sleeping, his dog repeatedly licked his face. Half-awake, he ignored it at first, but the dog was very insistent about waking him up. Larry did wake up and instantly smelled gas. The dog had saved his life. Only the dog had died a year earlier.

Some people are convinced that their animals play other roles after death. For example, the deceased pet somehow "sends" a new animal into the bereaved person's life, because it "knows" the person needs this companionship. Some people also believe that a pet who has died has been reincarnated into their new pet. There is no way to prove or disprove such beliefs.

Is Your Child's Grieving Excessive?

Expect that a grieving child will cry, lose his appetite temporarily, and act despondent. But after several weeks and certainly after months, you should start seeing improvement. If you're worried that your child is overreacting to the death of a pet, ask yourself these questions:

1. Is the anguish over losing a pet continuing to cause the child to do poorly in school, compared with her past performance? After the pet's death, many children will not do as well in school because of their grief, but improvement should occur eventually.
2. Is your child continuing to refuse to play with friends or to engage in activities that were formerly enjoyed?
3. Do you think that this grief is basically "taking over" your child? Are the usual things that you do to comfort your child just not working?
4. Is your child reacting similarly to how other children of the same age act? Read the section in this chapter on how children of different age

groups may react to the loss of a pet. If your child's reaction is more extreme than other children of the same age, and if the child does not appear to be getting better, you may need to seek professional help.

If you do decide your child needs professional help, you don't necessarily have to consult a child psychiatrist or psychologist. The school counselor may be able to talk out the problem with the child. Or a clergyperson may be able to help him resolve the grief and pain. Of course therapy with a mental health professional may also be needed.

When Is A Child Ready For A New Pet?

Parents should pay attention to the signs that a child may be ready for a new pet. For example, if you take the child to a mall and the child shows interest in looking at the animals in the pet store, this is a sign that they may be ready to choose a pet at your local animal shelter. Shelter animals usually receive all their immunizations and the cost may be free or minimal. But more importantly, you are likely saving a life when you adopt a pet from an animal shelter. (Chapter 12 also addresses issues related to whether you're ready to acquire a new companion animal.)

The next chapter discusses issues related to when disabled and/or elderly people lose a beloved pet.

Chapter 10

People With Special Needs: Disabled People And Elderly People

D ealing with your pet's death can be particularly difficult when you are a disabled person and your pet has assisted you for years. But even if your pet is not a formal guide dog, hearing dog or other type of assistance animal, and instead, your pet is a "plain old" dog or house cat, you may be largely housebound because of a disability and as a result, you have become very attached to your companion animal.

In addition, if you are an elderly person whose children are fully grown and you have already lost many friends, including animal friends, your recently deceased pet may have provided you with much needed love and companionship, and her death can be particularly painful to cope with.

When A Service Animal Becomes Sick Or Dies

Because animals have a shorter life span than humans, disabled people must face the loss of their animal companion and the acceptance of a new one. This poses a problem of practicality—the disabled person must adapt to a new animal companion, regardless of whether or not they've finished grieving over their previous one.

Also, if the animal cannot function as a service animal anymore because of illness, the disabled person may believe mistakenly that somehow it is his or her "fault." This is an idea that others should help to refute.

One Man's Story

Jimmy, who has a mental disability, relies on his dog Summit when he becomes confused. But Summit has cancer, and Jimmy says his dog's illness has forced him to think about what life without his animal companion might be like. Though his coworkers and friends have raised nearly enough money to pay for a needed operation for Summit, Jimmy worries.

He says, "I still may lose him. But it has helped so much to have the help and affirmation of friends and strangers around me, fighting to keep him alive and working. If I should lose him, I know that there are many around me who will grieve the loss with me. I was most afraid of being alone with that grief."

Experts say that disabled people whose animal provided assistance to them suffer the same kinds of grief as nondisabled people when the animal sickens or dies. Of course, some people are more strongly attached to their animals than others, but within the range of reactions, virtually all who lose a helping animal suffer from the shock of having to deal with their disability again on a very basic level until they accept a replacement animal. Now they must cope again with limitations that they had forgotten about, even something as simple as picking up something dropped, an act that the dog always performed. Some people have likened the loss of the animal to becoming newly disabled.

Sometimes people feel like their service animals are irreplaceable. The person forgets that the animal had to be trained and that both the animal and the person had to go through a learning process of adjusting to each other—that first dog did not automatically know how to get to the person's workplace, how to find the way home from the bus stop and how to perform other learned tasks. (This is often a problem when a disabled person loses their very first assistance animal.)

Another problem arises when the disabled person chooses to keep the "retired" service or guide animal as a pet and acquire a new animal to perform the jobs that the "old" one did. One woman said that her older dog is very disabled with arthritis, but the dog is furiously jealous of the new dog, and will make a supreme effort to rush off to pick up something for her mistress.

The original dog clearly does not want the new dog to impinge on her own turf, even though it's extremely painful for her to accomplish these tasks. The owner feels very guilty seeing this, and says that she finds it is difficult to develop a good relationship with her new dog.

Because of the importance of a service or guide animal to a disabled person, it's a good idea to plan early on for what can be done when the animal becomes too sick to work anymore or dies. Some schools will not allow the person to keep a sick animal. Or if they do, they will refuse to provide another younger and healthier animal—it's one per person.

Elderly People Who Lose A Pet: Helping Them Cope

Animal companions can be very important to older people, improving their health and sometimes even giving them a reason for living.

Many older people dote on and love their pets, and the loss of their pet can be extremely traumatic. The elderly person may have already faced many losses—of friends and family as well as of key abilities, such as hearing or vision or mobility. In addition, the knowledge that a pet is dying or has died may force the elderly person to consider his own mortality.

The elderly person who sees his pet as the primary (or even sole) nurturing being in his life is the most at risk for severe grieving. On the other hand, it should be noted that sometimes older people are more adept at dealing with their grief, primarily because they've gone through it before. They may previously have lost friends, a spouse, and family members.

The problem becomes most difficult when the elderly person is isolated and/or is living alone and the pet may have been the only being they loved and who loved them back.

The companion animal is also someone to talk to and many caretakers frequently talk to their pets. Moreover pets provide older people with a sense of order and routine. Since they are usually retired and don't have to comply with a regular schedule, many older people need the sense of orderliness, the reason to get up in the morning, that a companion animal provides.

It's also interesting to note that older people with pets are more likely to pay attention to their health, perhaps because they feel responsible for someone other than themselves.

Worry Over A Pet May Prevent Seniors From Seeking Medical Care

Experts say that often older people are afraid to go to see their physician because the doctor may require hospitalization. And who would take care of the pet in that case? Family members and relatives should be aware of this fear and help the older person plan for it.

In addition, it's also a good idea to have the person carry a card with the name of their pets and instructions on who should be called in the event that the elderly person becomes ill or some emergency occurs. The possession of this card alone could give peace of mind to an elderly person and make him or her more willing to seek out needed medical attention.

Older People In Nursing Homes

Sometimes older people are placed in a nursing home and the staff and their relatives think that they are having problems adjusting to a new place, not realizing that the loss of their pet could be exacerbating the problem. Their pet may not have died, and may be under the care of a relative. Or the family may have chosen to euthanize an older pet when the elderly person needed to move to a nursing home, causing distress to the elderly person.

Nursing-home administrators should ask new residents if they ever had a pet and allow them to express their feelings. Talking does help. Some experts recommend asking questions about companion animals on preadmission forms. If the staff knows that the new resident is upset about the loss of a pet, they can help with the grieving process.

In some cases, nursing homes are actually bringing in pets for residents to enjoy on a regular basis. Administrators have discovered that the residents are happier and healthier when they have the pet's visit to look forward to.

Getting A New Pet For A Senior

If living circumstances allow for a pet, the older person may wish to adopt a new pet. For example, assisted living centers may allow pets, although they charge extra per month for the animal. The decision to acquire a new pet after grieving for a deceased pet can be especially hard for an older person, who may worry that they will be unable to care for the animal through its life. One solution is for the older person to find an older animal, usually at the local humane society or pet shelter. Acquiring an older pet from a shelter can also save an animal's life.

In the next chapter, the traumatic situation of runaway pets and other involuntary separations from pets are covered.

Chapter 11

Other Losses: Involuntary Separations And Runaways

S ometimes you have to leave your animal—or the animal leaves you. Your pet is (you hope) still alive out there, but the separation is nonetheless painful for you.

You may have to leave your animal because you're moving to a new place where they don't allow pets. Or you may develop a severe allergy to your companion animal, or perhaps you marry a person who is severely allergic to the type of pet who lives with you. Or in the worst case, your beloved animal may harm someone else and you may be forced to order him euthanized. Your animal companion may also run away and despite your best efforts, you never find him again. These are just a few of the situations in which you may be separated from your pet.

When You Must Move Away And The Pet Can't Go With You

According to researchers E. R. Shore and colleagues in their 2003 article for the *Journal of Applied Animal Welfare Science*, moving is the most frequent reason for giving up a pet. Often a new landlord will not allow pets. In a phone interview with 57 people who relinquished their animal companions, most felt compelled to give up their pets because of a move due to a new job. Despite an often strong attachment to the animal companion, external pressures overrode these concerns.

In an earlier study in 1999 that was also published in the *Journal of Applied Animal Welfare Science*, John C. New, Jr. and colleagues found that moving was the most common reason for relinquishing dogs to an animal shelter in the United States in a sample of 321 dogs. However, they found that it was the third most common reason for relinquishing cats (in a sample of 225 cats), after the reasons of the owners saying they had too many animals and that household members had allergies to the cat. Another common reason for the relinquishment of both dogs and cats was a landlord refusing to accept pets.

Because of changed circumstances, including a reduced income, aging, or maybe a conscious decision to cut back on expenses, you may find that you must give up your companion animal. You know that if you take an older animal to the animal shelter, it may or may not find a family (and if not, your pet may be euthanized). Or maybe you plan to stay in your residence, but you just cannot care for a companion animal anymore. Circumstances like becoming ill may make caring for your pet too great a responsibility.

Retiring A Pet

Sometimes a larger animal must be retired because of his or your personal circumstances. Darlene told me that it was very painful to retire her horse, and she said, "I think that anytime you go through a change with an animal, whether it is euthanizing a pet or sending your horse to a retirement home, you want to make sure that you are in full touch with all your feelings about it."

She continues, "I retired my thoroughbred last week and was as upset about that as I would be if he had died. Some people asked me how I felt as the trailer drove away. Well, I was driving the trailer. I wanted to be the one who took him to his new home. I wanted to let him go and run and have a ball. He loved it and is very happy. I am the one who is in mourning for my loss of this lovely guy."

When Your Pet Disappears

In some ways, the disappearance of a pet can be worse than its death. Although you hope to get her back, you also know that you may never see her again. Realistically speaking, you really don't know if your pet is sick or scared and you may wonder if she was stolen. Your imagination can create many frightening scenarios. And if you, an adult, can conjure up such thoughts, then think of what your child may imagine!

You feel as if you can't really grieve until you know the truth. You're stuck in an ambiguous situation, as if your pet were missing in action in a war. As a result, the "denial" stage of grief is extended beyond its normal duration. You may also be very angry at yourself for your own (real or imagined) negligence and you may be angry with the pet as well.

Children, especially younger ones, may become especially fearful because they often identify with their pets. They may suffer from a fear of loss or abandonment if a pet disappears, and may worry about their role in the world, which is no longer seen as a safe place. They may express concern and fear when despite their best efforts, their parents can't solve this problem. If parents can't find a beloved pet, will their parents be able to protect them? Plenty of reassurance and TLC is indicated in such cases.

When your pet is missing, create signs or posters and hang them up around the neighborhood and in shop windows (with the permission of the owner, of course). It's a good idea to provide as specific a description as possible: type of animal, breed, coloring, name, approximate weight, and any distinguishing characteristics. If you can provide duplicate photos, so much the better.

Go to houses and apartments in your area and ask everyone if they've seen the pet. You may also choose to advertise your missing pet in the local newspaper.

Call the local animal shelters. Maybe someone brought in your pet, and you definitely do not want the animal taken by another family or, worse, euthanized.

Check "lost and found" ads in the local newspapers. It's possible you may find your pet there.

You may wish to offer a reward for the discovery and return of your pet to you, in both posters that you display and newspaper advertisements. Don't be overly lavish with the reward amount: Check what others are offering for in similar situations.

You may get crank phone calls, so if anyone calls about the pet, don't let your children take the call. If it sounds like someone really has found your pet, arrange to meet him outside his house or a parking lot or possibly outside your house. Do not let strangers in your house.

Unfortunately there are thieves who will steal your pet and then seek a reward for returning the animal to you. You will probably be so grateful that you won't care. However, if you suspect that you are being victimized, contact your local police. This is important because if the scam works with you, the criminal will try it with other distraught pet owners.

When is it time to think about finding a new pet? This subject is covered in the next chapter.

Chapter 12

When Should You Think About Adopting A New Pet?

fter my dog died and then within a year, my beloved cats also died, our family did not have a pet for several years. Then one day, I asked my grandson Tyler if he thought we should get a cat. He said, "That would be a miracle!" We discussed it with Grampa and then we all decided to look at photos of kittens and cats on the local animal shelter's website.

We actually were thinking about adopting one particular cat because her photo was so beautiful. But when we arrived at the shelter, a scrawny little kitten kept trying to attract our attention by loudly meowing, leaping about, sticking her claws out of the cage, and doing everything she could think of to attract notice, finally succeeding. That cat was Fluffy, a happy healthy cat, and she chose us. She was also an abused cat—someone had twisted her tail when she was a tiny kitten and broken it. But other than having a short tail, she is fine. We all think that we (or she?) made the best choice ever.

After your pet dies, some well-meaning people may tell you to rush out and obtain a "replacement" animal. If you feel certain that this is a good idea, then do so; however, most experts recommend you wait at least a month from when your animal companion died before adopting a new pet. You need to be emotionally ready and you also need to realize that your new pet won't be interchangeable with your previous one. And if you're not ready for a new pet right away—and many people are not—don't let anyone pressure you into adopting one.

One problem with rushing into adopting a new pet is that if you look too hard for a "clone" of the pet you have lost, you will almost inevitably be disappointed. Even animals of the same breed can have different personalities and "Rex" and "Rex Two" are bound to be very different.

When people instantly replace a loss, they may do so because they think that they can avoid suffering from grief. The problem with this reasoning is that it often backfires.

Pet lovers and experts say that it's a good idea to love an animal for itself, not for what it symbolizes to you—which is the lost pet. If your new pet can't live up to your memories of the pet that died, then you may be very disappointed and your new pet may not receive the love and attention it needs and deserves.

Ava was traumatized when her bird died in a sudden accident. She wanted a new bird but felt guilty about it. So she and her husband decided they would seek out an injured bird that they could nurse back to health—rationalizing that this is what the bird that died would have wanted. They went to a pet store and discovered an ailing bird that the pet-store owner gladly gave them. In this way, they satisfied their need for a new pet with their equally pressing need to honor the memory of the one they had loved and lost.

When you do decide that it's time to adopt a new pet, consider your local animal shelter, which is likely full of many cats, dogs and many other animals who need a new home. If they can't be placed in a new home within a timeframe determined by the shelter, then the animal will likely be euthanized because many shelters simply do not have room for all the new incoming animals and the non-adopted animals who are already there.

How Do You Know When You're Ready?

Some animal lovers say that you'll know if and when you're ready for a new pet. For example, you may find yourself driving by the shelter run by the local humane society. Said Debbie, "I waited until 1 could go into the humane society without bursting into tears, and until another wonderful little puppy reached out and grabbed my heart the way Marty had when I first saw him."

You may also find yourself noticing other people's pets as well as looking with interest at photos or articles of animals in the paper that need a new family—and a spark of interest is generated. Or you notice ads for animals on your Facebook page and they look very appealing to you. Maybe that particular animal isn't for you, but you start thinking about what it would be like to live with a new pet.

Issues To Consider Before Choosing A New Pet

Many people who decide that they need a new pet will choose the same species as their pet who died (a dog, cat, lizard, etc.), and they may stick to the same breed as well. You should ask yourself several questions before you automatically search for the same kind of pet as you had before.

- Has your lifestyle changed? For example, if your former pet was a lively terrier, can you still keep up with a high-energy dog—or would a more sedate dog be better for you?
- Have your living circumstances changed? Maybe you've moved to an apartment and it would be difficult to care for a large gregarious pet like your animal companion who died. Or maybe you've moved from the city and out to the country and the big dog you've always wanted would be happy here.
- Have your children grown up? Maybe you chose your last pet based on what you felt the children needed or could handle. If they are grown and gone, what kind of pet do *you* want?
- How much care can you provide? Do you want a high-maintenance pet or one who is more independent?
- Is your neighborhood safe for walking a pet? If you don't want to walk your animal at night, you should choose a cat, hamster, rabbit, or even a small dog who can be trained to use newspapers that you've laid out.
- Do you have many visitors and an active social life? If many people come to see you, along with their children, then you want a pet that is friendly and outgoing and who won't have to be locked up every time that visitors come to your home.
- Are you an active person? If you are active and athletic, or at least you get out on a regular basis, an animal that enjoys the outdoors would be a good choice for you. But if you are a sedentary person who spends

lots of time indoors, your normal lifestyle will make an active pet very unhappy.

- Do you want a baby animal or a more mature pet? Sure, baby animals are very cute. They also require a lot of training and patience. A more mature animal might be a better choice for some families.

- Do you have severe arthritis or some other disabling condition? If so, an extremely active pet that needs a lot of outdoors time may not be right for you. You could consider a small mammal, fish, or bird.

- Are you at home much or away from home a lot? Some animals need plenty of attention, so if you're not home very much, you should not select such a pet. In addition, some breeds of pets need a lot of grooming and care, so take that factor into consideration. For example, if you are considering a cat, you may choose to get a shorthair cat if you won't be around much to do the daily brushing and grooming that longhaired cats require.

- Do you have any allergies to animals? If you are allergic to cat dander but you still want a cat, a shorthaired cat would be a better choice than a longhaired cat. Or you may choose to get another type of animal altogether.

- Do you have a home business? Some people might be annoyed by animals jumping on the computer, the fax machine and other devices or knocking over their supplies. (My cat periodically turns off the answering machine by jumping on the phone. But I've learned to live with it.)

- Do you have other pets? Some animals do better as the "only child" while others can get along fine with your other animal companions. Don't assume that a new animal will be immediately accepted by your other pets, despite their past positive relationship with the pet that died.

- Do you have an infant or toddler? Choose a pet that likes children and who can tolerate the tail-pulling and pushing that they may receive at the hands of curious children. Be sure you don't choose a pet that would be likely to retaliate by biting.

These are only a few suggestions. Be sure to also ask the animal shelter or the person from who you adopt the pet for as much information as possible on the kind of animal that you are thinking of bringing into your home. Try to find articles on the Internet or books in the library on a particular breed or type of animal before you make your decision.

Introduce New Pets Slowly To Old Pets

Maybe your cat and dog were inseparable and then the cat died. You should get a new cat as a friend for the dog, right? Not so fast. Animals have their own personalities and the new pet may not be a welcome addition—at least, not at first.

Experts advise that rather than bringing in a new pet permanently, caretakers introduce the animal to other pets. For example, you could try having a friend bring in the animal and ignore it yourself. Let the older pet have a chance to meet the new animal, without becoming jealous of attention you give to it. Sometimes this is just not possible. But if you can make it happen, use this strategy.

Some People Choose To Go Petless After A Beloved Pet's Death

Although many animal lovers will eventually obtain a new pet, there are others who feel that they can't go through all the work and pain of caring for an animal and the eventual grief of facing the pet's death. If they are fixating on the negative aspects of pet care, it is not a good idea to pressure them.

What If Someone Gives You A New Pet And You're Not Ready?

Many people have faced the situation in which someone who knows they've lost a beloved pet decides they really need a new one and gives them a pet as a surprise. They don't understand the nature of pet grief.

If you are not ready for a new pet, the best thing to do is explain that you can't accept the pet and then refuse to accept it. It's better for there to be some hurt feelings than for you to take on a responsibility that you don't need or want. No matter how hard you try, you may be unable to relate, and this is unfair to the new animal.

Your friend may be able to return the pet or may be able to find the animal another home, and maybe you could help—although it is not really your responsibility. If you are worried that the animal will be euthanized if you turn him down, you could call the local humane society or shelter and discuss the likelihood of finding the animal a good home. Be sure to explain the situation very clearly.

Conclusion

One sad fact that most pet owners must face is that our companion animals usually will not live as long as we do, and as a result, we will have to face their deaths. It's a painful thought, and also painful for our partners and our children. And yet by planning ahead for the inevitable, and by accepting death when it occurs as best we can, we can bring meaning to it all and honor our pets who have died.

Many people don't understand the extreme sadness that is suffered by many pet owners whose animals die. These people may not be animal lovers or they may, in their hearts, truly understand, but be afraid or embarrassed to admit it. It's okay to grieve! It's natural and it's normal.

I hope that this book has provided you with the understanding that grief is something that needs to be accepted and acknowledged, not hidden away. With such acknowledgment can also come acceptance and remembrances of past joys with your companion animal.

I hope that you have gained some coping tactics, and that they will work for you. Sometimes one of the hardest parts of facing difficult situations is thinking that you are the only one who has ever felt this way. Know that you are not alone.

If no one in your extended family is sympathetic and understanding, there are others out there who you can talk to. It might be your neighbor, or it could be a total stranger on a telephone hotline or a website online in another state or even in another country.

If your companion animal who has died could speak to you, I believe that he would be proud of the caring and love that you showed through your grief and would want you to remember him and also to carry on. I hope that the information provided in this book can in some measure enable you to achieve that goal.

About The Author

Christine Adamec is a freelance writer and the author of more than 40 books, including many encyclopedias on health issues such as diabetes, kidney disease, drug abuse and other topics. She is also the coauthor of *Fibromyalgia for Dummies* (Wiley, 2007). The underlying common denominator behind all of her books is a desire to provide helpful information to the people who need it. Check out her website at www.christineadamec.com.

Appendix A: Organizations That May Help

American Society for the Prevention of Cruelty to Animals (ASPCA)
424 E. 92nd Street
New York, NY 10128
(212) 876-7700
www.aspca.org

Association for Pet Loss and Bereavement (APLB)
PO Box 55
Nutley, NJ 07110
(718) 382-0690
http://aplb.org

Humane Society of the United States
2100 L Street NW
Washington, DC 20037
(202) 452-1100
www.humanesociety.org

International Association of Pet Cemeteries and Crematories
4991 Peachtree Road
Atlanta, GA 30341
(800) 952-5541
www.iaopc.com

The Latham Foundation
Latham Plaza Building
1826 Clement Avenue
Alameda, CA 94501
(510) 521-0920
http://latham.org

Pet Partners (formerly the Delta Society)
875 124th Ave NE, Suite 101
Bellevue, WA 98005
(425) 679-5500
www.deltasociety.org

Appendix B: Helpful Websites And Hotlines

Argus Institute for Families and Veterinary Medicine
www.argusinstitute.colostate.edu

Chance's Spot Pet Loss and Support Resources
www.chancesspot.org

Grief Healing
www.griefhealing.com

Hoofbeats in Heaven
(for those who have lost horses)
www.hoofbeats-in-heaven.com

Ohio State University
www.vet.ohio-state.edu/honoringthebond.htm
(614) 292-1823

Pet Loss Help
www.petlosshelp.org

Tufts University Pet Loss Support Hotline
(503) 839-7966
www.tufts/edu/vet/petloss/

University of Illinois College of Veterinary Medicine
www.cvm.uiuc.edu/CARE/
(877) 394-CARE

Appendix C: Listings Of Pet Cemeteries Nationwide

*Note: This is a partial listing of pet cemeteries in some states. Readers should thoroughly investigate these cemeteries and memorial gardens and their services before engaging them. Listing in this book is provided for information only and does not constitute an endorsement in any way. Some pet cemeteries have websites.

Alabama

Alabama Fairhope Pet Cemetery
21347 County Road 27
Fairhope, AL 36532
(334) 928-2603

Pets at Peace
1348 Highway 11
Trussville, AL 35173
(205) 467-7695

Arizona

Sierra Vista Pet Cemetery
East Ramsey Road
Sierra Vista, AZ 85636
(520) 378-2651

Arkansas

River Valley Pet Crematory and Cemetery
4201 Greenwood Road
Van Buren, AR 72956
(479) 474-7828

California

AA Sorrento Valley Pet Cemetery
10801 Sorrento Valley Road
San Diego, CA 92121
(619) 276-3361
www.svpc.biz

Bubbling Well Memorial Park
2462 Atlas Peak Road

Napa, CA 94558
(800) 794-PETS
www.bubbling-well.com

Los Angeles Pet Memorial Park
PO Box 8517
Calabasas, CA 91302
(818) 591-7037
www.lapetcemetery.com

Pet's Rest Cemetery and Crematory
1905 Hillside Boulevard
Colma, CA 94014
(650) 755-2201
www.petsrest.com

San Diego Pet Memorial Park
8995 Crestmar Point
San Diego, CA 92121
(858) 909-0009
www.sandiegopetmemorialpark.com

Colorado

Pets at Evergreen Memory Park
26624 North Turkey Creek Road
Evergreen, CO 80439
(303) 674-7750
www.petsatemp.com

Roselawn Pet Cemetery & Crematory
1706 Roselawn Road
Pueblo, CO 81106
(719) 542-2934
www.roselawnpueblo.com

Florida

Central Florida Pet Cemetery & Crematory
10505 SE 36th Avenue
Belleview, FL 34420
(353) 307-2256
www.cfpcc.com

Curlew Hills Memory Gardens Pet Cemetery
1750 Curlew Road
Palm Harbor, FL 34682
(727) 789-2000
www.curlewhillspetcemetery.com

Greenbrier Memory Gardens for Pets
3703 West Kelly Park Road
Apopka, FL 32712
(800) 257-2107
www.greenbrier.cc/index_memory_gardens.html

Pet Heaven Memory Park and Crematory
10901 West Flagler Street
Miami, FL 33174
(305) 223-6515
www.pet-heaven.com

Twin Oaks Pet Cemetery & Crematorium
251 NE 300th Street
Okeechobee, FL 34972
(863) 467-6377
www.twinoakscemetery.com

Georgia

Bi City Pet Cemetery & Crematory
7110-C Jamesson Court
Midland, GA 31820
(706) 569-6644

Memory Gardens for Pets
2571 Highway 441
P:O Box 1095
Watkinsville, GA 30677
(800) 925-6117
www.memorygardensforpetsga.com

Illinois

Hinsdale Animal Cemetery
6400 South Bentley Avenue
Willowbrook, IL 60527
(630) 323-5120
www.petcemetery.org

Paw Print Pet Cemetery
27 West 150 North Avenue
West Chicago, ILL 60185
(630) 231-1117
www.pawprint-gardens.com

Indiana

Forever Friends Pet Cemetery
9700 Allisonville Road
Indianapolis, IN 46250
(317) 849-3616
www.washingtonparkcemetery.org

Maryland

Aspin Hill Memorial Park and Pet Cemetery
13630 Georgia Avenue
Silver Spring, MD 20906
(301) 871-6700

Resthaven Memorial Gardens
9501 Catoctin Mountain Highway (US 15 North)
Frederick MD 21701
(301) 898-7177
www.resthaven.us

Valley Pet Cemetery and Crematory
127 Britner Avenue
Williamsport, MD 21795
(800) 962-1467
www.valleypet.net

Massachusetts

Angel View Pet Cemetery
471 Wareham Street
Middleboro, MA 02346
(508) 947-4103
www.angelview.com

Pleasant Mountain Pet Rest and Cremation Services
76 Liberty Street
Plymouth, MA 02360
(800) 852-0014
www.petrestofplymouth.com

Michigan

Noah's Pet Cemetery & Pet Crematory
2727 Orange Avenue SE
Grand Rapids, MI 49546
(616) 949-1390
www.noahspetcemetery.com

Sleepy Hollow Pet Cemetery &
Crematory
2755 64t^h Street SW

Byron Center, MI 49315
(616) 538-6050
www.sleepyhollowpc.com

Whispering Pines Pet Cemetery of Ypsilanti
943 Wray Court
Ypsilanti, MI 48198
(734-547-0083
www.whisperingpinespetcemetery.com

Minnesota

Hillside Pet Cemetery
6259 10th Avenue Southwest
Alexandria, MN 56308
(612) 763-6367

Missouri

Rolling Acres Memorial Garden for Pets
12200 North Crooked Road
PO Box 12073
Kansas City, MO 64152
(816) 891-8888
www.visitrollingacres.com

Montana

At Home on the Range Pet Cemetery
8400 Amsterdam Road
Manhattan, MY 59740
(406) 282-7378
www.athomeontherange.net

Nebraska

Rolling Acres Complex
400 South 134th Street

Lincoln, NE 68520
(402) 483-7001
http://rollingacrescomplex.com

Nevada

Craig Road Pet Cemetery
7450 West Craig Road
Las Vegas, NV 89129
(702) 645-1112

New Jersey

Abbey Glen Pet Memorial Park
187 Route 94
Lafayette, NJ 07848
(800) 972-3118
www.abbeyglen.com

New York

Hartsdale Pet Cemetery & Crematory
75 North Central Park Avenue
Hartsdale, NY 10530
(800) 375-5234
www.petcem.com

Memory Gardens Cemetery and Memorial Park
983 Watervliet Shaker Road
Albany, NY 12205
(518) 869-9506
www.memorysgarden.org

Pet Haven Cemetery
4501 West Seneca Turnpike
Syracuse, NY 13215
(315) 469-1212

Pine Rest Pet Cemetery
757 Seneca Creek Road
West Seneca, NY 14224
(716) 674-9470
www.pinerestpetcemetery.com

Rainbow Bridge Pet Cemetery & Crematory
146 Old Route 9
Fishkill, NY 12524
(845) 897-9710
www.rainbowbridge.com

Regency Forest Pet Memorial Park
760 Middle Country Road
Middle Island, NY 11953
(800) 372-PETS
www.regencyforest.com

Ohio

Boston Hills Memorial Park
7005 Walters Road
Hudson, OH 44236
(330) 653-6457
www.bostonhillspet.com

Karnik Memorial Garden
5411 Black Road
Waterville, OH 43566
(800) 820-6973
www.karnikmemorialgarden.com

Rome Pet Cemetery
1159 County Road 411
Proctorville, OH 45669
(740) 886-9888
www.romepetcemtery.com

Oklahoma

Precious Pets Cemetery
5510 North Spencer Road
Spender, OK 73084
(405) 771-5510
www.preciouspetscemetery.com

Pennsylvania

Crestview Pet Cemetery Animal Memorial Park
9915 Frankstown Road
Pittsburgh, PA 15235
(412) 731-7112

Greener Pastures Pet Cemetery
967 Griffin Pond Road
Clarks Summit, PA 18411
(717) 586-3700

Rhode Island

Rose Hill Pet Cemetery
Rose Hill Road
Peace Dale, RI 02883
(401) 789-1345

South Carolina

Pet Cemetery & Cremation Services
132 Red Bank Road
Goose Creek SC
(843) 797-5735
www.petrestcarolina.com

Tennessee

Cedar Hills Pet Cemetery
2467 Nashville Highway
Columbia, TN 38401
(615) 977-5524
www.cedarhillspets.com

Dixie Memorial Pet Cemetery
7960 Epperson Mill Road
Millington, TN 38053
(901) 873-0417

Texas

Faithful Friends Pet Cemetery & Crematory
3600 Shelby Road
PO Box 40581
Fort Worth, TX 76140
(817) 478-6696
www.ffpcc.com

Pets at Peace Pet Cemetery
1902 West Illinois Avenue
Midland, TX 79701
(432) 620-8677
www.petsatpeacecemetery.com

Smoke Rise Farm Pet Cemetery
11330 Mountain View
Azle, TX 76020
817-444-2221
www.smokerisefarmpetcemetery.com

Toothacres Pet Cemetery
1639 Parker Road

Carrolton, TX 75008
(972) 492-3711
www.toothacres.com

Utah

Cottonwood Canyons Pet Memorial Garden
3115 E. 7800 South
Cottonwood Heights, UT 84121
(801) 943-0375
www.utahpetcemetery.com

Virginia

Faithful Friends Pet Cemetery
6217 Memorial Drive
Sandston, VA 23150
(804) 737-6006

Noah's Ark Pet Cemetery
7400 Lee Highway-Hollywood Road
Falls Church, VA 22046
(703) 573-8800

Washington

Family Pet Memorial Gardens
20015 North Austin Road
Colbert, WA 99005
(509) 467-4248
www.familypetmemorial.com

Petland Cemetery
P.O. Box 184
Aberdeen WA 98520
(800) 738-5119
www.petlandcem.com

Bibliography

Adams, Cindy L., Bonnett, Brenda N. and Meek, Alan H. "Owner Response to Companion Animal Death: Development of a Theory and Practical Implications." *Canadian Veterinary Journal* 40 (1999): 33-39.

Adams, C.L., Bonnett, B.N. and Meek, A.H. "Predictors of Owner Response to Companion Animal Death in 177 Clients from 14 Practices in Ontario." *Journal of the American Veterinary Medical Association* 21, no. 9 (2000): 1303-1309.

Brandes, Stanley. "The Meaning of American Pet Cemetery Gravestones." *Ethnology* 48, no. 2 (Spring 2009) :99-108.

Buckley, Stephen A., Clark, Katherine A. and Evershed, Richard P. "Complex Organic Chemical Balms of Pharaonic Animal Mummies." *Nature* 431 (2004): 294-299.

Bustad, Leo K. and Hines, Linda M. "Relief and Prevention of Grief." In William J. Kay, et al., Eds. *Pet Loss and Human Bereavement*. Ames, IA: Iowa State University Press. 1984 Pages 70-81.

Carmack, Betty J. *Grieving the Death of a Pet*. Minneapolis, MN: Augsburg Fortress. 2003.

Harris, James M. "Nonconventional Human/Animal Bonds." In William J. Kay, et al., eds. *Pet Loss and Human Bereavement*. Ames, IA: Iowa State University Press. 1984 Pages 31-36.

Friedmann, Erika and Heesook, Son. "The Human-Companion Animal Bond: How Humans Benefit." *Veterinary Clinics of North America, Small Animal Practice* 39 (2009): 293-326.

Kaufman, Kenneth R. and Kaufman, Nathaniel D. "And Then the Dog Died." *Death Studies* 30, no. 1 (2006): 61-76.

Kimura, Yuya, Wabata, Hidenobu and Maezawa, Masaji. "Psychiatric Investigation of 18 Bereaved Pet Owners." *Journal of Veterinary Medicine Science* 73, no. 8 2011): 1083-1087.

King, Loren C. and Werner, Paul D. "Attachment, Social Support, and Responses Following the Death of a Companion Animal." *Omega* 64, no. 2 (2011-2012): 119-141.

Lagoni, Laurel, Butler, Carolyn and Hetts, Suzanne. *The Human-Animal Bond and Grief.* Philadelphia, PA: W.B. Saunders Company. 1994.

National Institute of Mental Health. *Depression.* Bethesda, MD: U.S. Department of Health and Human Services. 2011. Available online at http://www.nimh. nih.gov/health/publications/depression/depression-booklet.pdf (accessed September 20, 2012).

New, John C., Jr. et al. "Moving: Characteristics of Dogs and Cats and Those Relinquishing Them to 12 U.S. Animal Shelters." *Journal of Applied Animal Welfare Science* 2, no. 2 (1999):83-96.

Podrazik, Donna, et al. "The Death of a Pet: Implications for Loss and Bereavement Across the Lifespan." *Journal of Personal and Interpersonal Loss: International Perspectives on Stress & Coping* 5 (2000): 361-395.

Qureshi, Adnan, M.D., et al. "Cat Ownership and the Risk of Fatal Cardiovascular Diseases, Results from the Second National Health and Nutrition Examination Study Mortality Follow-up Study." *Journal of Vascular and International Neurology* 2, no. 1 (2009):132-135.

Rajewski, Genevieve. "Lifelines for Grieving Pet Owners." *Tufts Now.* August 6, 2012. Available online at http://now.tufts.edu/articles/lifelines-grieving-pet-owners (accessed September 15, 2012).

Shore, E.R., et al. "Moving as a Reason for Pet Relinquishment: A Closer Look." *Journal of Applied Animal Welfare Science* 6, no. 1 (2003):39-52.

Traisman, Enid, MSW. "Children and the Death of a Pet." DoveLewis Animal Emergency Hospital, Portland, Oregon. Available online at http://www.deltasociety.org/document.doc?id=690 (accessed August 18, 2012).

Walsh, Froma. "Human-Animal Bonds I: The Relational Significance of Companion Animals." *Family Process* 48, no. 4 (2009): 462-480.

Walsh, Froma. "Human-Animal Bonds II: The Role of Pets in Family Systems and Family Therapy." *Family Process* 48, no. 4 (2009):481-499.

Westgarth, Carri, et al. "Family Pet Ownership during Childhood: Findings from a UK Birth Cohort and Implications for Public Health Research." *International Journal of Environmental Research and Public Health* 7 (2010): 3704-3729.

Wrobel, T.A. and Dye, A.L. "Grieving Pet Death: Normative, Gender and Attachment Issues." *Omega* 47 (2003): 385-393.

Printed in Great Britain
by Amazon.co.uk, Ltd.,
Marston Gate.